CONTENTS

An Authentic American History

PURITANS'

A CATHOLIC PERSPECTIVE

PROGRESS

VOLUME
4

COMPILED BY THE EDITORS
OF ANGELUS PRESS
MATTHEW ANGER
PETER CHOJNOWSKI, PH.D.
MICHAEL MANCUSO
REV. FR. KENNETH NOVAK

1922 – 1941

The End of the Beginning

ANGELUS PRESS
2918 TRACY AVENUE, KANSAS CITY, MISSOURI 64109

ANGELUS PRESS
2918 Tracy Avenue
Kansas City, Missouri 64109
Phone (816) 753-3150
Fax (816) 753-3557
Order Line 1-800-966-7337

ISBN 0-935952-35-7 Series
       0-935952-39-X Volume 4

FIRST PRINTING—January 1996

Printed in the United States of America

ISOLATION AND THE RISE OF FASCISM
1922-1933

THE ROARING TWENTIES

The post-war world (and these United States, which formed an important portion of it) are inscribed in our cultural memory. The Charleston, bathtub gin, raccoon coats, jazz, Betty Boop, "Bright Young Things," and much beside have all contributed to an image of wild frivolity and sudden liberation. There was, to be sure, some truth to this notion, but only some.

The experiences of the War had led many to question the accepted beliefs of their raising, as ever war will. The ideas of *Sigmund Freud,* the Viennese psychologist who claimed that all mental illness was the result of sexual repression (this is a crude oversimplification, to be sure, but it adequately represents what many people *thought* Freud was saying) weakened the morals of many, and gave justification to many more who were looking to have them weakened.

The gaining of the vote for American women signaled the arrival of the "New Woman." Self-reliant, wise-cracking, equal to men in every way, the New Woman bobbed her

hair, shortened her skirt to her thighs, and flattened her figure, all the while smoking cigarettes. From the ashes of the
Gibson Girl of the 1890's emerged, phoenix-like, the Flap-
per. Hard-drinking and hard-living, she embodied the "Jazz
Age," as the era was called. In the wild abandon of the Charleston, she found her element.

Prohibition, intended as it was to cure drunkenness by
outlawing demon rum, had in fact the opposite effect. For a
whole new class of criminals arose, the bootleggers, to provide America the alcoholic relief she required. Although some
of this activity was undertaken by light-hearted amateurs
out for fun, bootlegging established such organized crime
figures as *Al Capone.* Rival gangs in cities like Chicago fought
for control of liquor-sales and gambling, shooting one another and buying off police and politicians. The Mafia came
into its own, and an element of lawlessness entered into
American life which had not been seen since the settling of
the frontier, and which has not yet left it.

The growth of the automobile, the radio, and the movies contributed to national conformity, while post-war prosperity gave a feeling of excitement to the big cities. During
the Twenties, Hollywood emerged as a center of entertainment, and Valentino led his short but wild career. Writers
and actors of a leftish cast thronged New York's Greenwich
Village, while nearby Wall Street boomed. It was the age of
F. Scott Fitzgerald, Damon Runyon, and *Thorne Smith.*

But in the midst of all the fun, darker currents flowed.
The revolution in Russia, horror at the horrors of war, fear
of the labor movement, and more such events caused not
only fear of Communist infiltration but a hatred of all things
foreign. In 1921 and 1923, laws were passed virtually elimi-
nating immigration from abroad. This, however, hardly affected "furriners" already here. To combat their influence,
the Ku Klux Klan revived; it had been founded in the early

1870's to terrorize Southern blacks, some of whom were given positions of power in the former Confederate states during reconstruction.

Just as big in the North as the South, the newborn Klan disliked foreigners of all sorts, blacks, Jews, and of course, Catholics. A delicate rhyme of theirs from the era sums up their opinions in the latter case:

> I'd rather be a Klansman, in robes of snowy white,
> Than be a Roman Catholic, in robes as black as night.
> For a Klansman is an American, and America is his home;
> But a Catholic owes allegiance to the Dago Pope of Rome.

So great was their power and influence in the early '20's that President Harding himself (ever a joiner of groups like the Elks and the Red Men) was initiated into the Klan in the White House. So too was a future Supreme Court Justice named *Hugo Black*.

The '20's, however, were far from being a pure amalgam of gangsterism and Klansmen. Perhaps the most representative figure to emerge from the period's literature was Babbitt, from the novel of the same name by *Sinclair Lewis*. A resident of the "up-and-coming" Midwestern town of Zenith, Babbitt was held up as an example of the loss of individuality and creativity supposed to result from thinking solely about business, the Rotary Club, and conformity. The word passed into English; "he's a real Babbitt" still implies that a person is at once a boor and a bore.

Babbitt was a proud descendant of the Puritans, at least in spirit. 1920's criticism kept up a continual barrage against the hapless Puritan, albeit often for the wrong reasons. H. L. Mencken continued to lambaste the "Booboisie," as he referred to the Babbitts and Puritans, first in the pages of *The Smart Set*, and then from 1924 to 1933 as editor of the *American Mercury*. His trenchant criticisms of the follies of the day remain excellent examples of fine essay-writing.

Mencken was one of thirty-three contributors to a 1922 collection of essays edited by **Harold Stearns**, entitled *Civilization in the United States:*

> Page after page detailed a shallow community life, the absence of democracy, the lack of fit between techniques and ideals, a culture that failed to engage the best minds, and a business-dominated civilization that sanctioned acquisitive materialism. Although in his introduction he denied a muckraking intent, Stearns drew three major indictments. First, the ideals and practices of the culture did not coincide, producing not a general feeling of hypocrisy but a fear of being found out. To this sure sign of decadence Stearns added the widespread delusion that the nation was predominantly Anglo-Saxon. Since Stearns used "Anglo-Saxon" as a term of derision, a synonym for dull, predictable, stodgy, limited, and repressed, the pretense of cultural uniformity by his lights had disastrous consequences for valuable diversity. Finally, Stearns saw social life as "emotional and aesthetic starvation, of which the mania for petty regulation, the driving, regimenting, and drilling, the secret society and its grotesque regalia, the firm grasp on the unessentials of material organization of our pleasures and gaieties are all eloquent stigmata. We have no heritages or traditions to which to cling except those that have already withered in our hands and turned to dust. One can feel the whole industrial and economic situation as so maladjusted to the primary and simple needs of men and women that the futility of a rationalistic attack on these infantilisms of compensation becomes obvious (Daniel H. Borus, ed., *These United States*, p.19).

These criticisms were echoed in various ways by the contributors. Interestingly enough, where Lewis was considered a liberal, Stearns was deemed conservative. He was in any case a product of Harvard, and a school of criticism which had developed there about 1910; this was the much bally-hooed "New Humanism."

Led by such men as the ironically named *Irving Babbitt*, *Paul Elmer More*, *Norman Foerster*, and *Robert Shafer*, the New Humanists considered that every civilization needed to strive for the ultimate good (although they could not agree as to what that was—Babbitt, for example, seeking refuge in a kind of neo-Buddhism). Art, so long as it was oriented toward that good, had moral authority in a culture. The New Humanists believed in what they called "Classical" restraint, as against "Romantic excess." While Mencken lampooned them mercilessly, they did influence one other important figure besides Stearns, *T.S. Eliot.*

Heavily influenced by both Babbitt and Santayana, Eliot emigrated to Great Britain in 1914. There he attempted with *Ezra Pound* and others to develop a new sort of poetry; this was called *Modernism* (not to be confused with the heresy of the same name). His 1922 poem, *The Waste Land*, relying as it did on both an ultra-contemporary mode and the symbolism of the Holy Grail, was seen by many as a perfect mirror of modern man's condition. Others were not so impressed. However that may be, Eliot's conversion to Anglo-Catholicism and taking British citizenship in 1927 completed the process begun when he left the St. Louis of his birth for the Boston of his ancestors. In later years he described himself as an Anglo-Catholic in religion, a Royalist in politics, and a Classicist in literature. In a word, he came in the conduct of his own life to disown the American ethos. His later friendship and admiration for *Charles Maurras* (of whom more presently), and avowed Papalism, completed this process.

Further South, some of the notions of the New Humanism affected the formation of a group of poets and critics at Nashville's Vanderbilt University just after World War I. The leader of this group, called the Fugitives after their magazine of the same name, was *John Crowe Ransom*. Associated with him were men like *Donald Davidson, Andrew Lytle, Merrill Moore*, and *Robert Penn Warren*. Originally, these men protested against the "backwardness" of Southern culture. But as the '20's progressed, the Fugitives, like so many others of the time's artists and writers, began to protest against the materialism and crassness of the contemporary American life they saw to be given over to the pursuit of profits–ignoring all religious and aesthetic aspects of life. They began to re-examine the history and culture of their own region, which would come to appear as one which had, at great cost to itself, resisted domination by the industrialized and money-oriented North.

In that north, however, in Providence, Rhode Island, dwelt a writer named *H.P. Lovecraft* (1890-1937). Lovecraft was a pioneer in the writing of horror fiction; his strange short stories dealing with odd entities and decaying New England towns appeared from 1923 on, primarily in the pulp magazine *Weird Tales*. He too shared a dislike of the materialism and cheap boosterism prevalent in his day, and sought refuge not only in horror, but in contemplation of the traditional lore and customs of New England (all the while both condemning Puritanism, the American Revolution, and various other stand-bys of that tradition). Although he claimed to be an agnostic materialist for most of his life, his letters show an increasing sympathy for Catholicism which one may hope bore fruit.

Richmond saw the arrival on the scene of a similarly inclined figure, fantasy writer *James Branch Cabell* (1879-1958). Cabell set most of his novels in the fictional French medieval province of Poictesme. While he avoided the use of realism, his work showed a dark view of the human condition.

All of these writers had in common a deep distrust of and disillusionment in what they considered to be the materialism and sheer crassness of the life of the nation; added to this was a rejection of the national cult of progress, itself a secularized version of Calvinistic predestination. But during the 1920's, while there were pockets of poverty, to be sure, the general prosperity rendered all such complaints seemingly inaccurate. After all, if the majority prospered under the current system, what were all these criticisms save the whinings of maladjusted and alienated intellectuals? Only mass disillusionment, of the sort that financial ruin brings, would give the protests of the intelligentsia any hearing amongst the majority of Americans. Otherwise, such complaints against a system which, whatever its faults, managed to provide a good living for the majority of its residents could not possibly be true. Could they?

Between 1922 and 1925, the liberal magazine *The Nation* hired 48 writers of varying opinions and backgrounds, from Mencken to pro-Communist Johan J. Smertenko, to write articles on each of the states. From these can be drawn an intriguing picture of a nation in transition; transition, however, from bucolic boredom to industrialized conformity. Few of the writers were quite as nasty as Edmund Wilson in his description of New Jersey:

> But the smarter communities come even further from fostering an independent local life. It is either a question of well-to-do commuters who are fundamentally New Yorkers and who never really identify themselves with New Jersey as citizens of that State or of people with country houses who merely come down to New Jersey for a few months in the summer. And they do not even carry smartness to a particularly brilliant point. Rich brokers and powder manufacturers build houses like huge hotels, where their families go about the familiar busi-

ness of motor and country club. There are the regular tennis, golf, and polo, and, occasionally, a half-hearted fox-hunt. Scattered fragments of a local squirearchy live in the country all the year round, accustomed to the society of their horses and dogs and not greatly missing any other. The children of both these elements, rather unusually stupid flappers and youths, pursue a monotonous round of recreation of which they never seem to tire. They are neither very sprightly nor very wild and between the beach club, the tennis club, and the country club attain a sun-baked, untroubled comeliness of healthy young solid animals. They have not even much of a heritage of snobbery to give them the distinction of a point of view (Borus, *op.cit.*, p.244).

While Wilson was perhaps more snappish than was usual among his colleagues, his sentiments were echoed in most of the articles. From C.L. Edson's jolly observation of his native state that: "Arkansas has its own popular motto and it is this: 'I've never seen nothin', I don't know nothin', and I don't want nothin'.' These fundamental aims the people of Arkansas have achieved in every particular"; to Leonard Lanson Cline's maintaining that Michigan had gone from being "...without identity, without community of purpose or past, without tradition..." to taking on an air "...of newness, of hardness, of thin varnish, faking up what passes for prettiness," in a word, to becoming the "...consummation of the salesman's ideal;" the same themes are played upon. Alongside these, of course, were coverage of local questions like the control of Montana by the Anaconda Copper Co. or of Delaware by the du Pont clan. Yet, in the dreary picture so painted, a few locales were looked at as islands of sanity. San Francisco, New Orleans, and Baltimore were highly commended by their assigned authors for their having escaped the deadness of the rest of the nation. The reason for this, so it was said, was the close connection of those towns to Europe; we might say, even if they would not, to cultural Catholicism.

HARLEM RENAISSANCE AND THE FIRST BLACK POWER MOVEMENT

New York City, however, remained the Great City of America. Center of theater, of publishing, of trade and commerce, on the little island of Manhattan was encapsulated the whole of the American experience from the penthouses of Park Avenue to the tenements of the Lower East Side. One of the city's most well-known areas between the wars, however, was newly black Harlem.

Before World War I, Harlem was a primarily German settlement which had been engulfed by New York City as the metropolis, during the course of the 19th century, crept up the island and spilled over into Westchester County (eventually annexing the region called The Bronx). But after the War, Harlem underwent a great change.

Many blacks had come North during World War I from the impoverished South, exchanging the grinding life of poor sharecropping for the grinding life of factory work. After the War, many more made the trek, leaving behind the poverty and post-Reconstruction Jim Crow laws for the chance to make real money and to live with fewer restrictions (and, so they hoped, less prejudice). In Chicago, Boston, Philadelphia, and many other major Northern cities, black neighborhoods or ghettos developed. The best known of these was Harlem.

To Harlem came black artists, musicians, writers, and intellectuals from all over the nation. Many of these had served in the army during the war and were exposed to the relative color-blindness of French society. Returning to an

America where the newly re-emerged Ku Klux Klan had singled them out with Catholics and Jews as enemies, and where anti-black riots and lynchings had taken place during and just after the war in several Northern cities (perpetrated mostly by white workers who feared an influx of cheap labor), such folk were understandably resentful. In Harlem they would attempt to carve out an enclave where the black man would come into his own.

In great part, Harlem between the wars fulfilled much of this dream. Mingling with poverty were black-owned businesses and newspapers; such places as the Cotton Club and the Apollo Theater figured strongly in the growth of jazz. Thereat would play such great names as *James P. Johnson*, *Willie "the Lion" Smith*, *Thomas "Fats" Waller*, and *Edward Kennedy "Duke" Ellington*. Singers and dancers like *Josephine Baker* (who would go on to be the toast of Paris), *Bessie Smith* and the Catholic convert *Billie Holiday* (who made her debut in 1931) were accompanied by them. To hear these performers, well-to-do whites came uptown to Harlem in the 1920's and '30's, dressed in their finery; one of the reasons "the Lady is a Tramp" in the song of that name is her refusal to go to Harlem "in ermine and pearls."

But achievement in Harlem was not restricted to music. This was the era of the *Harlem Renaissance*. Prior to the 20's, books about black life and culture were written primarily by whites, employing a great deal of dialect—like *Joel Chandler Harris's* Uncle Remus stories. But the writers of the Harlem Renaissance wrote about these topics as insiders; further, they did not depict their topic as an amusement, but in an attempt to foster pride among their co-racialists. In one sense, they were part of a large movement; the scientific study of American folklore in general dates from about this time, and as we have seen, regional writing was flourishing. But the fact of intelligent writers dealing with the situation of what remained basically a subject people was without parallel. That Jim Crow could easily survive when the majority of blacks were illiterate field hands and domestic workers was obvious; but in the face of articulate opinion, just how well could legal segregation and so on continue?

At any rate, the writers of the Harlem Renaissance were an interesting lot, indeed. Chief among them were *James Weldon Johnson*, best known as the author of the 1927 book *God's Trombones*, a presentation of seven sermons in free verse, showing the style and concerns of black preaching, a major element in the culture; *Claude Mckay*, a Jamaican immigrant poet and novelist (most notably 1928's *Home to Harlem*); *Countee Cullen*; and *Langston Hughes*. But perhaps the most remarkable was *Zora Neale Hurston* (1891-1960).

Hurston was the first black woman writer to achieve prominence in the United States; in her relatively short career she produced two books of anthropology (*Mules and Men* and *Tell My Horse*), four novels (one of which, *Seraph on the Suwannee*, represents perhaps the first time in a novel a black author wrote about white characters exclusively), a play, and an autobiography (*Dust Tracks on a Road*, perhaps the most incisive and rhetoric-free description of the black experience in America as yet written). Her work was excellent taken on its own merits, and portrayed people–black and white–sympathetically, but without either sentiment or animus. Without doubt she was one of the greatest writers this nation has produced in the 20th century.

All of the Harlem Renaissance writers had this much in common: they wished the black man to take his place in America alongside the white as an equal partner. But just as the Klan called for the separation of the two races, so too (for completely different reasons) did a black leader who rose to prominence in the Harlem of the 20's: *Marcus Garvey*.

Garvey, born in Jamaica in 1897, had founded in his native land in 1914 the Universal Negro Improvement Association (UNIA). Its aims were to foster black pride of race and economic power, and to reclaim Africa from the colonial powers; all blacks would return thereto, and an independent black nation would be established. Finding little support in Jamaica for these goals, Garvey arrived in Harlem in 1916. Within three years he had garnered 2,000,000 supporters in Harlem and the other Northern ghettos. That year of 1919, in order to stimulate black economic power within the white system, he founded Negro Factories Corporation and the Black Star Line of steamships. UNIA's businesses included restaurants, grocery stores, an hotel, and a printing press. Garvey's power was at its apex in 1920, when his international convention brought together delegates from 25 countries. The high point was a parade of 50,000 through Harlem's streets.

The next year he proclaimed himself president of the "Empire of Africa"; he went so far as to approve the Klan, precisely because it too favored the separation of the races. He soon feuded with established black leaders, like W.E.B. Du Bois of the NAACP. In 1922 he was indicted and convicted of mail fraud, receiving a sentence of 5 years, which was commuted by President Coolidge in 1927 to deportation. His movement did not long survive him.

The importance of this episode, however, is that it points up an enduring question of American racial relations–what is the goal toward which white and black Americans ought to strive for together? Separation or integration? Given that there is an inequality between the two races, and antipathy on either side, what is the proper role of government in dealing with the problem? Given also that the government does not operate under a clearly defined moral or religious code, how far should it be allowed to take charge of the question?

Above all, what does justice demand in this case? Unfortunately, these are questions which, while recurring throughout our history, seem as far from a solution today as ever.

THREE PRESIDENTS AND THEIR ADVENTURES

Warren Harding was an amiable man, if not too discerning. His associates, however, were not always of the highest caliber. Committed as he was to returning the nation to normalcy, Harding pursued a laissez-faire approach to business. So too did various of his cabinet secretaries. Most notable of these was Secretary of the Interior Albert B. Fall.

On May 31, 1921, Harding transferred control of the Naval oil reserve lands from the Department of the Navy to Fall's control. On April 7, 1922, Fall secretly granted control of the Teapot Dome oil reserves in Wyoming to Mammoth Oil Company head Harry F. Sinclair. Shortly after this, a friend of Sinclair's gave Fall over $200,000 (roughly 2 million today). Fall asked Papal Count Edward Doheny of California for a $100,000 non-repayable loan. Not long after, Count Doheny received leases of parts of the Elk Hills and Buena Vista reserves in his native state. Naval Secretary Edward Denby innocently signed all the transactions.

News of these shenanigans leaked out; Congress ordered President Harding to quash the deals, and nullified the transfer of the reserves from Navy to Interior, after the Supreme Court ruled against all of it. Fall was convicted of accepting a bribe, while Sinclair and Count Doheny were acquitted. Various other folk involved were imprisoned or committed suicide.

Harding was crushed by what he regarded as wholesale betrayal by his most trusted appointees. The public at large were shocked, and lost confidence in him. While no one

accused Harding himself of any wrongdoing, it was nevertheless clear that his laxity in monitoring his staff had been
partly to blame for the affair. While we have grown some-
what used to these sorts of goings on in high office, at that
time there had been nothing like it since the days of President Grant. The effect on public trust, coupled with all of
the Prohibition-related events (which featured so many local
officials in the pay of bootleggers) contributed to a tremendous breakdown in public life.

Exhausted and broken-hearted, Harding died in the midst
of a national tour at San Francisco on August 2, 1923. Stay-
ing at his father's farmhouse in Plymouth, Vermont, Vice
President *Calvin Coolidge* was awoken in the wee hours of
the morning; his judge father administered the oath of office to him, and Coolidge became the 30th President of the
United States.

The new chief executive was the very picture of a stern
old Puritan father. Thin and harsh-appearing, he looked, in
the words of Alice Roosevelt Longworth, as though "he had
been weaned on a pickle." He was felt by his new electorate
to encompass all the virtues of thrift and frugality summed
up in *The Old Farmer's Almanac*. Although his Party was
rent by factional strife, the administration was stained by
scandal, and Congress was in rebellion, he moved swiftly
and quietly to exert control. He was easily nominated by the
Party in 1924.

Using the motto, "keep cool with Coolidge," he was re-
elected, announcing in his inaugural address that "the business of America is business." As president (save for Latin
America, as we shall see) his method in both foreign and
domestic affairs was nonintervention. For the former reason, he refused to join in any "entangling alliances" in Europe; for the latter, he opposed both a bonus to World War
veterans, business regulation, and farm relief.

The name "Silent Cal" was earned through keeping his public statements to a minimum. The story is told of a female reporter who informed him that she had a bet with the others in her office that she could get him to say more than two words. "You lose," was his reply. Similarly, upon his return from church services one Sunday, he was asked what had happened.

"The preacher preached."

"What about?" asked his wife.

"Sin."

"What did he say about it?"

"He was against it," came the magisterial reply. Coolidge won musical renown, of a sort, when the hit '20's song, *Crazy Words, Crazy Tune*, included the immortal line, "You all heard, yesterday, what did President Coolidge say? Vo-do-de-o-do-do-deo-do!" Rarely in history has a leader so well matched his time and his people.

For the '20's were a time of change and excitement, and in such times, we Americans always look to a father figure. What silent Cal performed would be done again by a much more active figure shortly after his term ended. In any case, so long as Calvin Coolidge was on the job, Middle America (a phrase which can mean either the Midwest, the Middle Class, or whatever bedrock group one wants to mention) felt relatively unthreatened by changes in society, by the upward spiraling credit cycle, and even by the gangs which were coming to have so much power in places like Chicago and New York—to say nothing of the political machines which dominated them.

But storm clouds were gathering, and Coolidge did not intend to face them. In 1928, he informed the Republican Party Convention that "I do not choose to run again..." This led to the nomination of *Herbert Hoover*, who had served in many capacities, most notably as organizer of famine relief to Allied Europe during and after the Great War, and as chairman of the Colorado River Commission; through his work, Hoover Dam was built. Hoover squared off against the Democratic nominee, New York Governor *Alfred Emmanuel Smith*. First practicing Catholic ever to be nominated for the presidency, Al Smith was called "the Brown Derby," after his habitual head-gear. Apart from this, he was outspoken in his opposition to Prohibition; worse yet in a country which still to a large degree suspected urban life, Smith was a New Yorker's New Yorker.

A product of the city's long-notorious *Tammany Hall* system, Smith was nevertheless renowned as being scrupulously honest. Easy-going and straightforward, he knew how to work a political machine without selling his soul to it. In 1926, Broadway habitué and composer *Jimmy Walker* won election as mayor of New York on Smith's recommendation. The Brown Derby had become the best known Democrat in the nation, and favored to win nomination in '28. As soon as this became well-known, the assault on his religion began.

In August of 1926, the president of the New York Anti-Saloon League, Methodist Bishop Adna W. Leonard of Buffalo, declared: "No governor can kiss the papal ring and get within gunshot of the White House" (*New York Times*, August 9, 1926). After handily winning at the 1928 Convention, Smith had to endure continued attacks on his Faith:

> [Smith's Catholicism] far outweighed every other issue in the campaign. There was a long history of anti-Catholicism in American politics. It was always a powerful force at the polls. Even an impressive old Progressive like William Allen White was upset by Smith's nomination: "The whole Puritan civilization which has built a sturdy, orderly nation is threatened by Smith."

The Protestant churches led the attack on the governor. It was not unusual for a church to try to influence American politics. The Baptists in the South and the Methodists in the North had been major political instruments for more than a century. And six months before the Houston convention, a Methodist Bishop, James Cannon, was touring the South trying to organize an anti-Smith bloc to deny him the nomination. On the eve of the election the *Memphis Commercial Appeal* carried an advertisement urging, "Vote as You Pray." At the request of the Republican National Committee, Mabel Walker Willebrandt, assistant attorney general, went to Cincinnati to address a gathering of Methodist ministers. Hoover had studiously avoided any mention of religion. Mrs. Willebrandt, however, was carried away by the sight of 2,000 divines at her feet. "There are 2,000 pastors here," she exulted. "You have in your charge more than 600,000 members of the Methodist Church in Ohio alone. That is enough to swing the election" (Geoffrey Perrett, *America in the Twenties*, pp.313-314).

It is interesting to note, in looking at this passage, that there was no question of "separation of Church and State," to be found here. Catholics, as we shall see, were accused of desiring to break this separation; but of course, it did not really exist, save when convenient for the enemies of the Faith to evoke it:

> Then, too, there was the matter of Smith's religion. Stronger even than the agrarian myth in America was the Protestant myth. According to it, the United States always had been and must forever remain a dominantly Protestant country. Never before Smith's time had a Catholic seriously sought a presidential nomination. Anti-Catholic prejudice was an old American heritage that dated back to colonial times and had flared up again with every major accretion of Catholic immigrants. To most Americans religious prejudice was principally a

matter of feeling rather than of reason, but with Smith's
candidacy some intelligent questions began to be raised.
Would a Catholic President of the United States owe a
double allegiance, to a foreign potentate, the Pope of
Rome, as well as to the American nation? Would he be
free to support such fundamental principles as the equality
of all religions before the law, the separation of Church
and State, and the American system of free public schools?
Debate on these subjects reached a high plane in two
Atlantic Monthly articles of 1927, one contributed by
Smith himself, who asserted eloquently that his church
loyalty left him free from any of the restraints alleged or
implied and denounced with fervor the injection of the
religious issue into politics. But only those were convinced who wished to be convinced, and Smith's nomination brought out anew every scurrilous anti-Catholic
charge that had ever been made. Particularly in the South,
where Protestantism was still militant, Smith's religion
cost him many votes (John D. Hicks, *Republican Ascendancy 1921-1933*, pp.206-207).

If America was Protestant, then of course allegiance to
Methodism or Baptistery implied nothing more than adherence to the spiritual side of the American ethos. But if it was
not, then surely such adherence implied a double allegiance
just as great as that of Catholics vis-à-vis the Pope. Today,
when believing Protestants are as much a minority in the
country as Catholics, we see the logical result: Evangelical
Christians who run for office are similarly accused of the
same "crime" with which their fathers charged Al Smith.
Equality of religions before the law, separation of Church
and State, and the public schools, these principles which the
Catholics were accused of wishing to destroy, have been the
means of driving all religion—indeed, morality, from public
life. Hence, one might say that their preservation has done
little for those who considered them in 1928 to be dogmas

of the true national religion. At any rate, the course of the campaign was very dirty, indeed. Robert Leckie well describes it, as well as Smith's reaction:

> One of the chief reasons for Al Smith's defeat was the vicious and sometimes obscene attacks made upon him by the Klan and similar nativist groups. Much of the old literature of No-Popery was reprinted and circulated, and it was charged, among other things, that after President Smith handed the United States over to the Pope, His Holiness would issue a decree bastardizing all non-Catholic children. [In Catholic folklore there is a probably spurious but nevertheless very funny anecdote which claims that after Smith was defeated he sent the Pope a one-word cablegram which said: "Unpack."]. If this were not absurd enough, there were actually people who expressed their alarm that the tiny ceremonial cannon outside Georgetown University was pointed directly *at the Capitol.* Unfortunately, in minds disposed to think ill, nothing is too ridiculous to be believed, and much of this arrant if scurrilous nonsense was taken for truth. In fact, Governor Smith himself complained that the Republican Party was not above issuing campaign literature "of a nature other than political." Smith's remark came during his celebrated speech in Oklahoma City. Aware that Southwestern states such as Arkansas and Oklahoma were particularly frenzied in their hostility, so much so that there was "real concern for Smith's personal safety" in Oklahoma City, he courageously decided to beard the lion in his den and bring the religious question into the open.

> "I have been told," he said, "that politically it might be expedient for me to remain silent upon this subject, but so far as I am concerned no political expediency will keep me from speaking out in an endeavor to destroy these evil attacks."

The first myth which Smith demolished was the charge that as governor of New York he appointed practically no one but Catholics to office. "What are the facts?" he asked. "On investigation I find that in the cabinet of the Governor sit fourteen men. Three of the fourteen are Catholics, ten are Protestants, and one of Jewish faith. In various bureaus and divisions of the Cabinet offices, the Governor appointed twenty-six people. Twelve of them are Catholics and fourteen of them are Protestants. Various other State officials, making up boards and commissions, and appointed by the Governor, make a total of 157 appointments, of whom thirty-five were Catholics, 106 were Protestants, twelve were Jewish, and four I could not find out about." What Smith could but did not add was that in New York State was located the country's largest concentration of Catholics, and that his co-religionists had not fared quite so well under him as under non-Catholic governors. Having gone on to detail other examples of bigotry in his campaign, Smith concluded:

I here emphatically declare that I do not wish any member of my faith in any part of the United States to vote for me on any religious grounds. I want them to vote for me only when in their hearts and consciences they become convinced that my election will promote the best interests of our country. By the same token, I cannot refrain from saying that any person who votes against me simply because of my religion is not, to my way of thinking, a good citizen...

The constitutional guaranty that there should be no religious test for public office is not a mere form of words. It represents the most vital principle that ever was given to any people. I attack those who seek to undermine it, not only because I am a good Christian, but because I am a good American and a product of America and of American institutions. Everything I am, and everything I hope to be,

I owe to those institutions (*American and Catholic*, pp.291-292). [Emphasis added.]

Here, in a word, was the tragedy of Al Smith, and of American political Catholicism in the 1920's. For as we see, the accusations against Smith and American Catholics in general were completely false. No single group were more committed to the secular faith of the country than were the Catholics–although this meant tacitly abandoning everything in the Church's social teaching which might clash with the American secular cult.

By their tactics, we have seen that even the self-appointed watchdogs of American liberty did not believe in it as much as the Catholics did. This is unfortunate indeed, because, after all, they are now as much that cult's victims as are the Catholics. Had Catholics in politics remained firmly committed to the principles of such Papal encyclicals as Gregory XVI's *Mirari Vos*, and Leo XIII's *Immortale Dei* and *Rerum Novarum*, the heirs of Smith's Protestant opposition in 1928 might not be a universally reviled minority in the 1990's.

Had that been the case, however, it is doubtful that Catholic politicians could have obtained anything like the influence which they did. There would have been no Smith campaign in 1928, and surely no Kennedy victory in 1960. But ballot-box victories for Catholics have done little for either Church or State in this country. If, perhaps, all that energy had been put into the integration of Catholics' lives with their Faith (whence would have sprung a zeal to convert the nation), rather than merely getting them elected to office, there would have been much beneficial and fundamental change here: surely the only way of putting Catholic political principles into practice in the US is by making them a Catholic nation. What is saddest about the election of 1928 is that Smith, like most American Catholics, really and sincerely believed that, as may be seen by the first two sen-

tences of Leckie's quotation from his speech, "religious
grounds" and "the best interests of our country" could be
separated. In truth, separation of the two is like separating
soul from body—the exact definition of death, and one which
our present status seems to exemplify.

In any case, Hoover won handily. The only lasting result
of the campaign was to make the Italians and French-Canadians of New England, long staunch Republicans in opposition to the Irish-ruled Democrats, willing to vote with the
Irish. Catholics continued to conform politically, and, as we
shall see, frequently did so at the expense of their co-religionists.

THE CHURCH IN THE 1920's

Despite the opposition to Catholicism inherent in national life (and exposed once more for public viewing, as we
have just seen, in the 1928 election) in the 1920's the Church
continued to grow in this country. Although immigration
had slowed to a trickle, those who had arrived in the preceding few decades consolidated their lives in the new land,
building ever more grandiose and beautiful churches. Although Margaret Sanger (a fallen-away Catholic) had founded
the forerunner of Planned Parenthood in 1921, the vast
majority of Catholics in this country still agreed with Church
teaching on the matter—for the time being, anyway. As a result, the numbers of Catholics continued to rise through
childbirth. (Interestingly enough, the 1920 Lambeth Conference of all the world's Anglican Bishops condemned birth
control; that of 1930 reversed this position). There were in
addition some few converts made.

In truth, the material position of the Church in America
could not have been better. New orders of sisters were spring-
ing up to staff ever more schools and hospitals; many other

orders were imported. Catholic universities and colleges grew in numbers also.

Nor was spiritual life unaffected by all this growth. Devotion to St. Therese, the newly canonized Little Flower, spread rapidly; sodalities and confraternities of all sorts were founded. Holy Name Society Communion Sundays, the early First Communions advocated by Pope St. Pius X, numerous choirs inspired by the *motu proprio* on Church music issued by the same Pontiff, and all sorts of other efforts were evidence of this.

The crowning achievement of the American hierarchy in this decade was, without doubt, the financial rescue of the Holy See by Chicago's Cardinal Mundelein in 1928. The signing of the Lateran Treaty with the Italian government the next year would obviate any need for further loans from American bishops—at least for a while. But a precedent was established.

Yet under all of this apparent prosperity, religiously and temporally, the Church in America was becoming ever more Americanist. The Bishops' Program for Social Reconstruction referred to in the last chapter, was tacitly abandoned, although the Catholic Central Verein in St. Louis continued as a strong voice for the Church's social teaching. *Fr. Joseph Husslein, S.J.*, among others, continued to labor to make the Church's doctrines in social, political, and economic matters well known. Two episodes illustrate in what direction the American Church was going.

The first was the Sentinelle Affair among the French Canadians in New England. The roots of the affair lay in France, where *Charles Maurras* had founded in the late 19th century an organization called *l'Action Française*. In his youth a positivist, his studies of history and literature convinced him that the Monarchy and the Church were what had built France's glory, and so must be restored to their former state if France were ever to again be the great nation it had been.

Although Maurras himself was for most of his life an unbeliever, all but a few of his comrades were fervent Catholics. Cardinal Billot, the Jesuit theologian, Cardinal Charest of Rennes, and Cardinal Dubois of Paris were all vocal supporters of the movement. Its influence was felt all over Europe, and such luminaries as *Hilaire Belloc*, *Arthur Machen*, and T.S. Eliot expressed their admiration thereof. Men like *Salazar* in Portugal, *Fr. Groulx* in Quebec, *Denis Jackson* in Australia, *Saunders Lewis* in Wales, *Stuart Erskine* in Scotland, *Fernand Neuray* in Belgium, and many others throughout the Catholic world were much influenced by *Action Française*.

In Quebec, the afore-mentioned Fr. Lionel Groulx founded a similar organization, called also *l'Action Française*, and inspired by Maurras' group, albeit in a Canadian context. Summing up this ideology, Fr. Groulx declared in the newspaper of the same name's January 1921 issue:

> Our doctrine can be contained in this brief formula: we wish to reconstitute the fullness of our French life. We wish to reconstitute in its integrity, the ethnic type which France left here and which one hundred and fifty years of history has shaped. We wish to remake an inventory of moral and social forces, which in itself will prepare their flowering. We wish to purify this type of foreign growth in order to develop in it intensively the original culture, to attach to it the new virtues acquired since the Conquest [of Canada by Great Britain from the French], above all to keep it in intimate contact with the forces of its past, in order to let it go henceforth its regular and individual way. And it is this rigorously characterized French type, dependent on history and geography, having ethical and psychological traits, which we wish to continue, on which we base the hope of our fu-

ture; because a people, like all living things, can develop only what is in itself, only the forces whose living germ it contains.

This germ of a people was one day profoundly strickened in its life; it was constrained, paralyzed in its development. The consequences of the Conquest weighed heavily upon it; its laws, its language were hamstrung; its intellectual culture was long hobbled; its system of education, deviated in some of its parts, sacrificed more than was fitting to English culture; its natural domain was invaded, leaving it only partially master of its economic forces; its private and public customs were contaminated by the Protestant and Saxon atmosphere. A distressing make-up has gradually covered the physiognomy of our cities and towns, an implacable sign of the subjection of souls to the law of the conqueror.

This evil of the Conquest was aggravated after 1867 by the evil of federalism. Confederation may have been a political necessity; it may have promoted great material progress; for a time, it may even have given Quebec a greater measure of economy. But it could not prevent the system from turning notable influences against us. Our particular situation in the federal alliance, the isolation of our Catholic and French province amidst eight provinces in majority English and Protestant, the imbalance of forces which ensued, sometimes increased by the hostile policy of some rulers, led federal legislation little by little towards principles or acts which endangered our fundamental interests. The political system of our country, such as it is by way of being applied, leads not to unity but straight to uniformity.

But Fr. Groulx was far from entirely negative; in the same article, he offered a way out of the dilemma:

For our intellectual élite we ask Roman culture and French culture. The first will give us masters of truth, those who furnish the spiritual rules, which make shine on high the principles without which there is no firm direction, no intangible social basis, no permanent order, no people assured of its goal. In the natural order, the culture of France, the immortal educator of our thoughts, will achieve the perfecting of our minds. And when we speak of French culture, we mean not in the limited sense of literary culture, but in the broad and elevated sense in which the French mind appears to us as an incomparable master of clarity, order, and subtlety, the creator of the sanest and most humane civilization, the highest expression of intellectual health and mental balance. And equally we mean not an initiation which leads to dilettantism or to alienation, but a culture which serves without servility, which safeguards our traditional attitudes before the truth, which become a real and beneficent force, will permit our next élite to apply itself more vigorously to the solution of our problems, to the service of its race, its country, and its faith.

For Fr. Groulx, as for Tardivel and Laflesche before him, the French-Canadians ought to have the goal of being "a Catholic and Latin people, of being absolutely and stubbornly ourselves, the sort of race created by history and desired by God." Moreover, whatever quarrels they might have between one another, the French-Canadians would serve as a sure defense in the struggle shared by Anglo-Canadians to prevent the Dominion from being absorbed by the colossus to the South: "The more we preserve our French and Catholic virtues, the more faithful we remain to our history and traditions, the more we remain the element impermeable by the American spirit, the strongest element of order and stability."

As might be expected, such an ideology found support among the French-Canadians of New England. A group of them launched in 1922 a newspaper, *La Sentinelle*, of

Woonsocket, Rhode Island, which was inspired by Fr. Groulx's thought, and whose editor was the redoubtable *Elphege Daignault*. In an American context, their program meant the safeguarding of French-Canadian religion and culture through the maintenance of national parishes and schools. When, in the mid-twenties, the Irish bishop of Providence, having appointed an Irish pastor to St. Louis Church in Woonsocket, demanded a financial assessment of French parishes for an English-language high school (in departure from previous practice), the struggle was on. Petitions, protests, pew rent strikes, and finally, a mass rally of 10,000 in Woonsocket culminated in a civil suit against the bishop; in response, the next year Bishop William Hickey excommunicated 62 Sentinellistes connected with the suit.

It was a struggle which divided Franco-American New England. Like the *ralliement* in France, which saw the French Church cut in two over Leo XIII's call for Royalist French Catholics to abandon their King and rally to the anti-clerical republic, so too did this battle pit two elements—national tradition and loyalty to the hierarchy—which had always been in accord, against each other. Just as some rallied behind the Sentinellistes, and saw compromise with the Bishop as a betrayal of the ancestors, their opponents among their co-nationals saw defiance of that same Bishop as the same treason. Of the two major organizations, the Association Canado-Americaine in Manchester, New Hampshire, sided with the Sentinellistes, and the Union St. Jean Baptiste with the Bishop. The struggle spread throughout the French communities of New England: Central Falls and Pawtucket, in Rhode Island; Manchester; and Worcester, Massachusetts. After the excommunications, it was threatened that a French-Canadian version of the Polish National Catholic Church would be set up. Another schism seemed imminent.

A mediatrix was found in the person of "Little Rose"

Ferron. A native of Sherbrooke, Quebec, Little Rose was a stigmatized mystic, whose cause has since been introduced at Rome. Accepted by the Sentinellistes as one close to God, she was able to convince them to make submission to the Bishop in 1929, after which the movement, for the most part, died away.

While its influence lingered (the fiery anti-assimilationist Wilfrid Beaulieu, a disciple of the Sentinelle, launched his Worcester paper *Le Travailleur* in 1931; this journal proclaimed the same message until it ceased publication in 1978, the year before Beaulieu's death) the end of the *Sentinelle* meant the end of independent Franco-American critique of the US system, and was a corresponding victory for the Americanists. This victory was echoed in Louisiana, where in 1918 the Catholic schools had banned the use of French by students, a move echoed a few years later by the state public schools. The year 1926 saw the closing of the last daily French paper in New Orleans.

The second great episode was the American Catholic reaction to the 1926 *Cristero* rebellion in Mexico, of which we shall see more shortly. For our present purpose, what counts is the welcome given by American churchmen to four emissaries of the Catholic Mexican revolt:

> The four anticipated great success; Eamon de Valera had successfully appealed to American Catholics for aid against Ireland's oppressors, and they would do the same on behalf of Mexico. But at their first stop, Corpus Christi, the bishop rebuffed them with the comment that people in his diocese didn't like Mexicans. In Galveston, the bishop took a ten-dollar bill from his wallet and gave it to Rene, ending the interview. Houston, Dallas, and Little Rock were much the same–they got twenty, thirty, fifty dollars. Sleeping outdoors at night and eating as little as possible to economize, they believed the north-

ern states would be different–de Valera had succeeded there. The Archbishop of St. Louis was outraged by conditions in Mexico as described by Capistran Garza; he gave one hundred dollars. At the next seven stops–East St. Louis, Indianapolis, Dayton, Columbus, Pittsburgh, Altoona, and Harrisburg–they got even less. In Columbus, the bishop expelled them from his residence without even hearing them out. In New York, without warm clothing, they nearly froze. Friends said Boston was promising. They went. There, Cardinal O'Connell examined their credentials carefully and listened without interrupting. Then, in a fatherly tone, he urged Rene to suffer patiently the trials God was sending and told him to urge those who had commissioned him to do likewise. He advised Rene to get out of the whole business, to look for a job; he would be happy to give him a letter of introduction to the Masachusetts Knights of Columbus, who might be able to help him find work (David C. Bailey, *Viva Cristo Rey!*, p.103).

At first sympathetic to the Cristero plight, prominent and wealthy laymen like Count Nicholas Brady and William F. Buckley, Sr., appeared disposed to aid their brother Catholics financially. But intervention by American bishops (as well as fear for American oil holdings in Mexico) put their sympathy to rest. As Bailey puts it, "The American bishops deplored the persecution in Mexico and extended hospitality to exiles and refugees; but they drew back in horror from the suggestion that they help bankroll a rebellion. Some, like Archbishop Drossaerts, might lambaste the [US] administration for supporting [Mexican anti-clerical President] Calles, but they would never dream of violating the neutrality laws. Knights of Columbus leaders and a few Catholic Congressmen protested vigorously and demanded withdrawal of US recognition; but, after their complaints had been duly lodged and reported in the press, and after State Department officials had explained to them that it would be unwise to take extreme action, they ceased their badgering" (*op. cit.*, p.308). Surely, this bland inaction in the face of the martyrdom of a neighboring Catholic nation is one of the most inglorious events in the history of the Church in the United States. But it shows what that Church had become by 1929. What is most pathetic is that, as we shall see, intervention by the US government on behalf of anti-Catholic factions remained as much a part of our relations with Latin America as it had been before. One would think that America's Catholics might try to change this, but, alas, they did not.

We need not be too surprised at this, given the lukewarm reception accorded in this country to *Quas Primas*, the encyclical of Pius XI establishing the feast of Christ the King. It was not, of course, the feast itself which was ignored, for it was immediately and grandly observed. Rather, it was the teaching of the encyclical on that Kingship itself which was politely allowed to drop down the memory-hole:

18. Thus the empire of our Redeemer embraces all men. To use the words of our immortal predecessor, Leo XIII: "His empire includes not only Catholic nations, not only baptized persons who, though of right belonging to the Church, have been led astray by error, or have been cut off from her by schism, but also all those who are outside the Christian faith; so that truly the whole of mankind is subject to the power of Jesus Christ." Nor is there any difference in this matter between the individual and the State; for all men, whether collectively or individually, are under the Dominion of Christ. In him is the salvation of the individual, in him is the salvation of society. "Neither is there salvation in any other, for there is no other name under heaven given to men whereby we may be saved." He is the author of happiness and true prosperity for every man and for every nation. "For a nation is happy when its citizens are happy. What else is

a nation but a number of men living in concord?" If, therefore, the rulers of nations wish to preserve their authority, to promote and increase the prosperity of their countries, they will not neglect the public duty of reverence and obedience to the rule of Christ. What we said at the beginning of Our Pontificate concerning the decline of public authority, and the lack of respect for the same, is equally true at the present day. "With God and Jesus Christ," we said, "excluded from political life, with authority derived not from God but from man, the very basis of that authority has been taken away, because the chief reason of the distinction between ruler and subject has been eliminated. The result is that human society is tottering to its fall, because it has no longer a secure and solid foundation."

True enough; but in an America engulfed by prosperity, the Pope's words seemed faint to the ear, indeed—and any attempt to implement them would inevitably arouse to fever pitch the forces which had made themselves obvious in the election of 1928. Rather than suffer such abuse, Catholic America burned incense before the social clichés of their countrymen.

THE UNITED STATES AND LATIN AMERICA

In 1922, American troops were on guard in Haiti, the Dominican Republic, and Nicaragua. In the first two countries, American troops had intervened to prevent European occupation at the orders of Woodrow Wilson. In 1924, the Dominican Republic was returned to local control, but another decade would follow before Haiti would be evacuated.

Nicaragua was a different story. There, after withdrawal in 1923, the pro-Catholic Conservatives under the leadership of *Emiliano Chamorro* rose against the Liberal govern-

ment. The revolt was successful; President Coolidge refused
to recognize the new regime. In the face of American opposition, the Chamorro government resigned and the country
lapsed again into chaos. Coolidge had the country reoccupied in 1925, and appointed the Liberal leader *Somoza* as
president.

But it was in Mexico (as usual) that the real nature of US
Latin American policy became manifest. The country had
suffered Revolution continually from 1910 to 1920. When
the dust cleared, a thoroughly anti-clerical regime was in the
saddle. In 1917 it passed a series of laws based upon the
French 1904 code. Religious orders were expelled, as were
all Spanish priests. Churches became the property of the State,
and religious rites confined to their interiors; outside of them,
clerical dress was not permitted. Schools, hospitals, monas-
teries, orphanages, and so on were all seized and given over
to other uses or sold.

While these laws were initially only half-heartedly applied, the ascension to power of Plutarco Calles in 1926 saw
their application made rigorous. In retaliation, the Vatican
ordered all Mexico's priests to cease functioning: if the State
wanted the churches, they could have them! But Mexico's
laymen were not far behind. The National League for the
Defense of Religious Liberty organized an economic boy-
cott–Catholics would not travel, nor buy anything but abso-
lute necessities. The loss of governmental revenue in terms
of sales and other taxes was tremendous. Yet Calles would
not relent.

After the expulsion of the Apostolic delegate in July, spo-
radic Catholic uprisings began to occur. The League, with
the tacit approval of the Mexican episcopate, began plan-
ning a nation-wide revolt. The Catholic political Party, the
Union Popular, decided to join them. Its leader, Anacleto
Gonzalez Flores, addressed the membership thusly:

I know only too well that what is beginning for us now is a Calvary. We must be ready to take up and carry our crosses....I, who am here responsible for the decision of all, feel a sacred obligation not to deceive anyone. If one of you should ask me what sacrifice I am asking of you in order to seal the pact we are about to celebrate, I will tell you in two words: *your blood*. If you want to proceed, stop dreaming of places of honor, military triumphs, braid, luster, victories, and authority over others. Mexico needs a tradition of blood in order to cement its free life of tomorrow. For that work my life is available, and for that tradition I ask yours. (Navarrete, Heriberto, S.J., *Por Dios y Por la Patria*, pp.123-125).

In early 1927, the revolt blazed throughout a dozen Mexican states. By the end of the conflict two years later, over 40,000 men had served in the ranks of the Cristeros, as they were called from their battle cry, *Viva Cristo Rey!*—"Long live Christ the King!" Despite lack of much weaponry beyond what they could capture from government troops, despite lack of funding from abroad, despite official US support of Calles, they fought on, nearly to victory.

The Calles regime replied with unspeakable atrocities. Perhaps best known of their victims was **Blessed Miguel Agustin Pro, S.J.** But for all the killing, more Cristeros emerged from the countryside. Nor, despite the support of the United States for the government, did the Cristeros initially go unheard by the Pope. Pius XI issued another encyclical, **Iniquis Afflictisque,** in which he declared (cap.27) that "...We can scarcely keep back Our tears, some of these young men and boys have gladly met death, the rosary in their hands and the name of Christ the King on their lips. Young girls too were imprisoned, were criminally outraged..."

While the fighting continued, most of the bishops left the country (although some, like the Archbishop of

Guadalajara, took to the hills with the Cristeros). Despite
the fact that by 1929, victory appeared to be in Cristero
grasp, Vatican Secretary of State Gasparri was anxious to come
to an accord with Calles. Using two Mexican bishops for the
task, through the mediation of American Ambassador to
Mexico Dwight Morrow, an accord was signed with the Calles
regime on October 11, 1929. A month later, Jose Manriquez
y Zarate, Bishop of Huejutla, addressed the faculty of
Belgium's Louvain University:

> The Mexican people, preserving the pure, integral
> faith of their fathers look on the Pope as the Vicar of
> Christ on earth. Knowing this fact the enemies of Christ
> were very astute to betake themselves to Rome in order
> to break the immovable wall of armed resistance. Very
> soon they had the satisfaction of seeing the people sur-
> render their arms at the first signal from the Pope. Those
> in the government who consented to a settlement of-
> fered all kinds of promises verbally but never afterward
> removed a single comma from the monstrous laws that
> have wounded Holy Church in Mexico and strangled
> the most sacred rights of men and society.

The rebellion collapsed. Priests who did not abide by the
settlement were to be suspended. The government treated
the accord as a surrender by the Church, and despite the
promised amnesty, mass executions of Cristeros went on spo-
radically, even as late as the 1950's. The churches were re-
opened, but the anti-clerical laws remained until 1991. Even
with their lifting, all church property built prior to 1991
remains in government hands. The ideology of the ruling
party has not changed since the days of Calles. The fact that
they are willing to abolish these laws merely indicates that
Catholicism is no longer a threat—which is certainly a re-
buke to us. We have in any case already seen what American
Catholic response to the Cristeros was at the time.

EUROPE AND THE RISE OF FASCISM

The smoking ruins of Europe were not magically restored by the Armistice on November 11, 1918. The Russian Civil War, a bloody conflict, indeed, had resulted not only in millions of atrocities and an atheistic inhuman regime coming to power in an ancient Christian land; it had also produced a stream of White Russian refugees, who soon became fixtures of society in London, Paris, Istanbul, Berlin, Buenos Aires, New York, San Francisco, Shanghai, Harbin, and many other cities across the world. Beyond this, temporary or abortive Red regimes repeated the atrocities of their prototype in Hungary, Slovakia, Bavaria and other parts of Germany. The new Soviet state was bent on world domination, for all that it was in terrible shape internally. In every country Communist cells were organized under the paternal eye of Moscow's Comintern—the Communist International.

The presence of the White Russians in so many cities ensured that news of what Communist rule would mean was widespread. The Red Scare of which we spoke earlier was not without justification, for all that it was ignorantly directed oftimes.

Communism appealed to many in Europe, particularly proletarians and intellectuals, whose beliefs in the certainties of pre-War religion and politics had been shattered. Prior to the War, it was assumed that the ruling circles in each nation knew best; this notion was shattered in the muck of the trenches, and the blood of the Eastern Front. All hope that existing abuses in society would be gradually ameliorated by imposition of Liberal progress was destroyed. The great urban mobs became seemingly living beings, ready to follow anyone who promised solutions. These the Communists claimed to have in plenty.

But the old politicians, the industrialists, the great land-owners, were not without resources of their own–with which they would be quite happy to reward anyone who could harness the power of the mob, and keep it away from Communism and from bloodshed.

The Church, for her part, surveyed the wreck with dismay. The first encyclical of the new Pope, Pius XI, *Ubi Arcano Dei Consilio*, published on December 23, 1922, well described the situation:

> 11. Public life is so enveloped, even at the present hour, by the dense fog of mutual hatred and grievances that it is almost impossible for the common people so much as freely to breathe therein. If the defeated nations continue to suffer most terribly, no less serious are the evils which afflict their conquerors. Small nations complain that they are being oppressed and exploited by great nations. The great powers, on their side, contend that they are being judged wrongly and circumvented by the smaller. All nations, great and small, suffer acutely from the sad effects of the late War. Neither can those nations which were neutral contend that they have escaped altogether the tremendous sufferings of the War or failed to experience its evil results almost equally with the actual belligerents. These evil results grow in volume from day to day because of the utter impossibility of finding anything like a safe remedy to the cures of society, and this in spite of all the efforts of politicians and statesmen whose work has come to naught if it has not unfortunately tended to aggravate the very evils they tried to overcome.

In such circumstances, millions of Europeans felt alienated from their leadership, from Capitalism, and from Communism as well.

Moreover, there was a spirit abroad in Europe, bred partly from the experience of soldiers in the War, and partly from the youthful idealism of high school and college students too young to have served themselves. In Germany, Austria, and Hungary, the onus of defeat lay heavily on these two groups; in Allied nations, veterans felt themselves short-changed in return for all their wartime sacrifices, and students objected to being ruled by the same "old men" who had made their fathers and older brothers serve in a point-less and bloody conflict. Everywhere, the ex-soldiers yearned for the unity, brotherhood, and sense of purpose they had experienced at the front, in the face of a dull, indifferent, divided peace-time country to which they returned. The students, on the other hand, thrilled at once by the adventures of the soldiers and by their own idealism, regarded the soci-ety in which they found themselves as stifling and mediocre. A vague, indefinable mysticism with a political edge devel-oped out of this, a search for exaltation and ecstasy which somehow would transform the shell of Europe into the green land of the past, the shining realm of tomorrow, or both at once. In a word, it was a form of Romanticism, produced from the War's killing of the smug Age of Liberalism—even as the original Romanticism was the child of the Age of Reason's death at the hands of the Revolution.

In every nation of Europe these elements produced move-ments which aimed to strike at Capitalism and Commu-nism alike; some were Catholic, most were not. Those which were not looked to find mystical fulfillment not in Christ but in the nation or the race. Authors have come to call some or all of the groups after the first of them to come to power in a European state (Italy) by the name *Fascism*.

To our own time, Fascism (with which, in America, we tend to lump German National Socialism—the Nazis) remains a powerful symbol of oppression, and a pejorative which may be leveled at anyone whom we dislike. The greatest estimate of those who met their ends at the hands of the Nazis is 11

million, a large number, to be sure. Inevitably, the Fascists
and Nazis are conjured up as examples of the ultimate evil.

One cannot help, however, but wonder why. Eleven
millions are a large number, to be sure; but Stalin alone was
responsible for the deaths of 25-30 million, to say nothing
of his predecessors and successors at the helm of the Soviet
Union. While the German concentration camps, which lasted
in their classic sense but five years and have been shut for
50, are continually evoked, the Soviet Gulag's seven decades
and recent closure have been forgotten. In China, where as
of this writing Mao's system remains in place, some estimate
as many as 200 million lives were snuffed out by command
of the Father of Chinese Communism. As of this moment,
that regime retains Most Favored Nation status with these
United States.

We shall not speculate, however. Suffice it to say that we
must look at Fascism not for its current symbolic value, but
as disinterestedly and impartially as we would be expected to
look at Soviet and Chinese Communism. Hitler ought not
repel us more (or less) than Stalin or Mao. That having been
said, let us consider the facts.

Firstly, let it be said that the different groups lumped
together as "Fascist" often did not have much in common.
Where the National Socialists considered Germans racially
superior, Italian Fascists believed that their nation's superior-
ity was strictly cultural. Where Nazis feared and hated Jews
on grounds of blood, the Romanian Iron Guard opposed
them for religious and cultural reasons—and the Italian Fascists, until World War II, did not oppose them at all. The
same variety of attitudes characterized every issue with which
such folk were concerned. The problem is neatly stated by
H.R. Kedward:

> The tempting conclusion may well be that there is no
> such thing as fascism, only a number of groups and parties

which showed similar characteristics but were really quite distinct. There would certainly be some truth in this view, but it would tend to ignore the conviction of most Fascists that they were part of a general movement designed to change not merely their own nation but the whole of society" (*Fascism in Western Europe 1900-1945*, p.5).

The same author accurately portrays the complexity of the issues involved:

> It is essential to see that the ferment of ideas presented here was the basis not only for Fascism but also for modern art and music, modern science and technology, the growth of psychology and a new theology. Fascist ideology was one particular synthesis made up of ideas which had a variety of influence. When it is analyzed and broken down into its component parts it is found to contain much that in a different setting would be excitable. For this reason the label "Fascist" must be carefully used and "potential Fascist" not at all, for may not a "potential Fascist" turn his violence into art, his rhetoric into the pulpit or his wish to control people into advertising? (*Op. Cit.*, p.7).

Kedward identifies several conflicting pairs of ideas from the synthesis of which he maintains that Fascism arose. Let us examine them in turn, and make our own judgment of each.

The first was the aforementioned conflict between Capitalism and Communism. As observed earlier, many Europeans felt that neither the greed and rapacity of the one, nor the Godless cruelty of the other, fitted either of them to be the guiding philosophy of a civilized nation. Such folk sought for a "Third Way" between the two. One of the commonest solutions to the problem of economic organization was called variously "Corporatism," "Syndicalism," or "Guild Socialism." While there were very many different variations thereof, all versions agreed in calling for representation of the people on a class or professional basis, rather than geographically, as was and is done in most of the world's Parliaments. There was envisaged the organization of "Corporations" or "Syndicates" in each trade, encompassing employers as well as workers. These in turn would be represented in a "Chamber of Corporations" or the like, which might either replace or supplement the existing legislature. Some variants of the notion took the medieval guilds as inspiration—due to the place of the Church in those organizations historically, some Corporatists converted to Catholicism, and many Catholics interested in social problems became Corporatists.

Another allied notion in Great Britain and the Commonwealth countries was "Distributism," the child of G.K. Chesterton and Hilaire Belloc. This called for the widest possible distribution of property and business among the people of a country: in place of large agribusinesses and industrial conglomerates, Distributists favored small farmers and local business. They too wished the restoration of guilds, and so also looked to the Church for inspiration. More concerned with questions of banking and money circulation was Social Credit, proposed by Col. C.H Douglas. It advocated taking control of the money supply out of the hands of the banks and putting it into those of the government. All of the advocates of these ideas opposed as well international banking and high finance. Corporatist economics were generally adopted as part of their program by Fascist parties. But not all Corporatists, etc., were Fascist. One general distinction was that non-Fascist Corporatists believed that the Corporations should be organic bodies, built up from the grass roots and to whom the government should bear some responsibility; Fascists, on the other hand, saw the Corporations as being regime-directed and controlled. Moreover, where Fascists saw the ideology of the party as the animating spirit of such institutions, their opponents preferred something else—often Catholicism. But the apparent resemblances in structure, as well as shared antipathy to international finance has led to many commentators lumping all Corporatists together as "Fascists."

The next dichotomy examined by Kenward is that of "Rationalism" versus "Irrationalism." These two are to be found in every heart, of course, but in the 19th century they assumed an ideological function. Order, authority, control—these were the earmarks of the historic European right. Men like Maurras, for instance, laid great stress on the need for order in the State, and maintained that the modern crisis was the result of these having broken down. Contrarily, irrationalists (ranging from Nietzsche to the Anarchists to Freud) charged that the structures of society, and indeed rational thought oppressed man; according to such theorists, only living for the self, and in the moment, with no regard for society's strictures, could provide true happiness. Beyond politics, this was a movement which declared that the human urge to unrestricted sex and violence was not an expression of his lower nature, but his higher. To a greater or lesser degree, this was an attitude associated with the historic Left.

These two notions were fused into one by Fascism. The Fascists managed to be at once the party of order and of violence, of restraint and revolution. In this, as in their economic policy, they achieved a secular transcendence of the traditional Right/Left division. (Only Catholicism *truly* transcends divisions.) This being so, large elements of virtually every strata of society could find a place for themselves in the Fascist spectrum.

Akin to this last was the division between civilized and primitive. Throughout the 19th century, one current of thought, often identified with the Romantics, like Scott,

Chateaubriand, and Novalis, looked to Europe's medieval past and folk present for inspiration. Identifying again with the historic Right, these saw the Continent as having abandoned a glorious past for a dry, spiritually dead present. Opposed to this was the idea of progress, of evolution. Applying Darwin's theory to political and social life, and associated with Liberalism and Socialism alike, this cult of progress looked to a hypothetical future as the goal. Here too, Fascism managed to be both at once; declaring itself to be at once rooted in the nation's or the race's past, it claimed also to be the party of the future, leading the community ever forward into a glorious new age. Yet what the party was uniting were essentially a pagan past and a Godless future; barbarism joined with scienticism. The Catholic ethos of Europe was almost entirely left aside.

Kenward's last opposition is that of the mass and the elite. Here too, the categories were associated with the traditional Right and Left. On the Right, it was held that monarchs and aristocrats had a God-given duty to rule. By virtue of blood and birth and training, they were most suited to governance. The Left, of course, believed (or claimed to) in the common man—Marx's teaching was allegedly intended to pave the way for mass rule. But here too, Fascism managed to combine the two. For the Fascists, leadership would rest in a single charismatic individual, who would wield all effective power in the state; his word would be law, like an absolutist monarch of the 18th century. But unlike a monarch, he did not owe his position to God (nor was he responsible thereto) but to the "spirit" of his people—he was, in a word, the incarnation of the folk he ruled. Opposition to him was not, therefore, a crime against God, but against the sovereign people (whose sovereignty, however, would only be exercised through the ruler; it neither protected nor legitimized any single individual of that people). Hence Nationalism became an important part of the Fascist mix. The influence of Nationalism spread through Europe, not only leading to the exaltation of existing nations, nor solely in ethnic conflict in the racial crazy quilt of Eastern Europe, but in the revival of such peoples as the Scots, Welsh, Bretons, Basques, and Flemings. Fascism's influence versus that of Christianity could be seen in how far each of these movements saw themselves as either a) an important part of the European quilt, or b) a good solely unto themselves, with the right to oppress or vanquish other nationalities. Here too, Fascism would substitute for the religious virtue of old-fashioned patriotism—love of country—a Nationalism which was neither religious nor really so much love of country as hatred of the foreign. Unfriendly observers have characterized such Nationalism as an attempt to persuade Europeans to regard their country or ethnic group in the same way that Americans do theirs.

At any rate, both traditional Right and Left found much to sympathize with in Fascism, and much to oppose. For the Left, the aspects of imposed order, of exaltation of the past, and of a ruling elite and leader were repellent. Right-wing criticisms of Fascism were the opposite: its love of violence, its belief in evolution, and its appeal to the masses all disgusted old-style Royalists and the like. What then, was Fascism? In the end, if we wish to characterize it one way or the other, its this-worldly emphasis, its basic opposition to Christianity must line it up alongside Marxism. But this is an identification neither easy to make, nor true of all groups commonly identified as Fascist (though certainly it was true of the Italian Fascists and Nazis). An interesting confirmation of this is the fact that often strongholds of Communism in Italy and Germany (the Po Valley and Saxony, for example), were staunchly pro-Fascist during the years of Mussolini's and Hitler's ascendancy, only to return to their prior allegiance after those leaders' demise.

Italy, after the War, was torn between Nationalists and Socialists in the Chamber of Deputies, and an extremely militant Communist Party, which appeared to be headed toward power. To prevent this from happening, Pope Benedict XV lifted the *Non expedit* (the decree forbidding Catholics to take part in Italian political life after the 1870 loss of the Papal States). Don *Luigi Sturzo*, a Sicilian priest, founded the Popular Party. Based firmly on Catholic social teachings, and advocating Corporatism, the *Popolari* won in the November (1919) election 99 of 508 seats in the Chamber of Deputies. The new party was second to the Socialists' 151 seats.

In the years 1919-1922, Socialist and Communist gangs worked to destabilize the country—intimidating and even murdering their opponents. Mussolini, himself an ex-Socialist who had broken with the Party over the issue of Italian intervention in World War I on the Allied side (which he favored), organized the *squadritisi*. Formed of veterans and students intent on saving their country from Communism and in revitalizing Italian life, these groups engaged the gangs of the Left in precisely the same manner. Public order began to break down all over Italy; the country seemed on the verge of total anarchy.

There then occurred the famous "March on Rome." On October 26, 1922, the Fascists began to occupy public buildings in different parts of Italy. The next day they began a mass movement on Rome, only to find out that King Victor Emmanuel III had appointed Mussolini as Prime Minister, with emergency powers. The Fascists were in control; yet they had not seized power—they had filled a vacuum.

Mussolini quickly eliminated Socialism, and began to alter the shape of the country's political structure. It must be emphasized that many of his measures were good in and of themselves: the Corporate restructuring of the economy, family protection laws, and repression of groups (like the Mafia and the Grand Orient) which had always been problems for the Church were in accord with the social encyclicals. But these things were not done out of a love of Christ and the neighbor, but rather out of a basically non-religious ideology. "Everything for the State" was Mussolini's motto. Certainly, the continued existence of the Popular Party would have allowed pressure to be applied to Mussolini, forcing him to emphasize the better parts of his program.

But guided by Secretary of State Pietro Cardinal Gasparri (disciple of Leo XIII's Secretary of State, Cardinal Rampolla, who was believed by some to be a Freemason) Pius XI was content to leave politics to the State, if the rulers thereof simply allowed the Church to pursue her mission unmolested. It appeared to the Pope that if the Popular Party continued, at once representing Catholic interests and opposing Mussolini, there would be much unnecessary friction. Since a priest led the party, and many more acted as local organizers, the answer was simple. On February 1, 1924, he forbade priests to belong to political parties. Catholic Action was to be entirely separated from the *Popolari*. Sturzo resigned from the party in July, whereupon it collapsed. Its founder went into exile. In return, Catholic Action was recognized by the government. Peace settled over the land, for the moment.

But it was only for the moment. Based on an essentially atheistic outlook, Fascism soon clashed with the Church on the educational front. While religious instruction had been reinstated in State schools, it was made optional in the higher grades, where the philosophies of Kant and Hegel were to be taught. The struggle heated up, and both sides were anxious for a solution to this as well as the Roman Question (the illegal occupation of the Papal States by the Italian government). 1928 became 1929, and the stage was set for a con-cordat, similar to the one Pius VII made with Napoleon.

This was a particularly beneficial arrangement for both parties. The Church received the independence of the Vatican (to which Mussolini had been prepared to give much more territory than was settled for); financial reparations for the lost Papal States; acceptance of Catholicism as the State religion; revision of things like the law of marriage in accordance with Church teachings; and numerous other items of that sort. Catholic Action was given official status, and in a flash of Papal honor, the Black Nobility (those Roman nobles who had continued to recognize the Pope as sovereign of Rome after 1870, as opposed to "Whites," who accepted the House of Savoy) were given Vatican citizenship. In return, the State received the blessing of the Church, and Mussolini the credit of closing a fault-line which had impeded Italy since 1870.

Yet, as subsequent events showed, Mussolini was not to be trusted. Still and all, the question must be faced. Given the anarchy into which Italy was sliding, and Communist revolution imminent in 1922, what are we to make of Mussolini's rise to power? It would be difficult to argue with the opinion of Arthur Cardinal Hinsley, Archbishop of Westminster, who would distinguish himself as a fervent opponent of Fascism:

> To speak plainly, the existing Fascist rule, in many respects unjust, is one example of the present-day deification of Caesarism, and of the tyranny which makes the individual a pawn on the chess board of absolutism. I say that the Fascist rule prevents worse injustice, and if Fascism—which in principle I do not approve—goes under, nothing can save the country from chaos: God's cause goes under with it.

It would soon be apparent, however, that if God's cause

would go under if Fascism did so, it would have a tremendous fight on its hands if Fascism succeeded.

Benito Mussolini was a forceful personality, who knew how to use radio and newsreels to unite and inspire his countrymen. He soon set the economy to booming, and restored confidence in government. Under his rule, there was an appearance of class unity, and the fear of Red revolution was dispelled.

In the meantime, the prosperity of the 20's had spread through most of Europe. In France, Great Britain, Spain, Czechoslovakia, Germany, and elsewhere, parties more or less committed to Liberal Democracy succeeded one another in office, while the majority of their citizens happily enjoyed enhanced standards of living, and docilely went to the ballot-box at the appointed times. It was a period when, as popular wisdom had it, Communism would be kept out of Europe by four factors: the Papacy, the British House of Lords, the *Academie Française*, and the German General Staff. Yet this was a stability which depended upon one thing—continued prosperity. In the meantime, however, every detail of the Jazz Age now reigning in New York (save, of course, Prohibition) was reproduced in the great cities of Europe. Thither fled expatriate writers like Hemingway and Fitzgerald.

Not everyone believed that the current situation could last. Devoted adherents throughout Europe of the Old Right or the New Nationalism looked at Mussolini's Italy, and dreamed of reviving their own nations in similar wise. In Vienna, Budapest, Madrid, Bucharest, and elsewhere small groups formed with the idea of adapting Fascism to their own traditions. These men and women varied much from one another—and from a mustered-out corporal in Munich, one Adolf Hitler who was, however, likewise a fervent admirer of *il Duce*.

BACK IN THE USA

How was Mussolini seen in the untouched-by-war-or-revolution United States? With few exceptions, throughout the 1920's, publications as diverse as the *Saturday Evening Post* and the *New York Times* endorsed both his takeover and his internal policies. He was seen as "the Man who made the trains run on time." Nativists applauded him for restoring Italian traditions (though an endorsement from Klan types could hardly be seen as bright mark for him!). The general run of folk viewed him as the savior of his country from Communism—this at a time when the United States were having their own "Red Scare." Above all, he was seen, at his worst, as a necessary evil, needed to force an indolent and ignorant people into the modern world. They would be impressed by all his posturing. Hard-working, hard-headed Americans, on the other hand, were supposed to have no requirements for national father figures and flashy dictators. They were a free nation of rugged individualists, full of republican virtue. Indeed, indeed. American freedom, rugged individualism, and republican virtue were all three shortly to receive their greatest test since the War Between the States.

The Boom of the 20's simply could not last; credit was highly inflated, and the mass practice of buying stocks on borrowed money, then repaying the loans with dividends, built an economic house of cards. In October, 1929, the bubble burst. On Black Monday, the New York Stock Exchange plummeted. Within a few weeks, stocks had lost 40% of their value. Prices fell, some wealthy and many middle class folk were financially ruined, and banks and industries failed. Thousands were thrown out of work; with every bank closure and industrial failure, the process accelerated. On the farm, runaway deflation destroyed the value of crops, while in those states affected by the Dust Bowl, it was the crops themselves which were destroyed.

In short order, this Great Depression, as it was called, sped round the world, spreading the same swath of economic destruction. This storm would challenge every government and every institution on earth; many would crack under the strain. In all nations, the system was severely challenged. It would be so in Europe and Asia, in Latin America and the British Dominions. It would be so in the United States.

A WORLD TURNED UPSIDE DOWN

The effect of the Great Depression on the world's peoples was catastrophic, not merely in an economic sense, but in a psychological one. Almost everyone everywhere, it seemed, was affected. As banks failed and businesses went bankrupt; as tumbling farm prices made beggars of the farmers and factory closures did the same for industrial workers, it seemed that the whole edifice of modernity was doomed. The complex structures of finance and industry, credit and bureaucracy which had emerged since the 19th century (and which were little understood by the masses of people who lived under them) seemed about to collapse. Never, perhaps, since the Barbarian invasions which brought down the Roman Empire had life seemed so fearful and bleak.

Despite this, however, two inventions emerged which brought the embattled folk of the 1930's much solace: commercial radio and sound pictures. Despite the atmosphere of gloom which pervaded both this country and the rest of the world, the Depression was in many ways the Golden Age of both media.

Radio brought a steady stream of news and entertainment into every home, directly linking the listener with the outside world. While this did much to end rural isolation in those places where electrification had taken root, it also bred discontent. One can only imagine the longing for the unattainable a family in say, drought-ridden Oklahoma, would feel listening to the glamorous sounds of Guy Lombardo and his Royal Canadians, "live from the Grand Ballroom of the Astor Hotel in New York City." Without a doubt, however, the Big Bands who are so legendary today were the creation of the combination of records and radio.

The medium lent itself to the production of radio plays; soon a never-ending stream of series—mysteries, comedy, soap operas, and the like were being churned out. From *The Shadow* and *The Whistler* through *Little Orphan Annie* and *The Easy Aces* to *My True Story* and *The Columbia Theater of the Air*, there were shows of every imaginable description. Being strictly audio, these programs made the listener a sort of co-creator, inducing him, through the use of sound effects, to conjure up in his own imagination the appearance of the action described.

Radio also revolutionized advertising, as various companies sponsored these shows in order to promote their products.

The advent of sound was revolutionary in the world of movies. Many an actor's or actress's career was ruined because, however appealing their appearance, their voices were unsuitable. But some did make the transition, and many more replaced those who could not. *Mae West*, *Frederic March*, *Errol Flynn*, *Clark Gable*, and *Myrna Loy* were only a few of the names who came to prominence in this period. In its infancy, the industry produced such classics as *Dracula, Robin Hood, Little Caesar,* and *Treasure Island.* Musicals were invented, wherein such as *Fred Astaire* and *Ginger Rogers* would transport their impoverished and despairing viewers into a never-never land of song, dance, and romance.

This was also the age of the Movie Moguls: men like *Louis B. Mayer* at MGM, *Darryl F. Zanuck* at 20th century-Fox, and *Jack Warner* at Warner Brothers produced some of the finest pictures ever made, but ran the industry like the Robber Barons of the 19th century. Big-name actors and moguls both were able to command wealth unheard of to most Depression-era audiences. Where old money and Industrial tycoons alike took pains to conceal their wealth from the impoverished crowds, Hollywood flaunted it. What would be intolerable activity on the part of a factory owner became expected in an actor: people loved to read and hear about the scandalous life-styles of the stars, and so a new kind of journalism was born–the Hollywood gossip column. The battling queens of the profession during the Depression were public enemies and secret friends, *Hedda Hopper* and *Louella Parsons*.

While all of this may seem a bit unimportant, it introduced into our culture an element which has been present ever since. The effect of entertainment media on molding societal attitudes has been enormous; at the same time, the influence is reciprocal, since the media must make a product that will sell. Nevertheless, what is portrayed onscreen approvingly is halfway to acceptance by the general public. The frequent divorces and other irregularities of some of the Stars contributed, in the long run, to legitimizing such behavior. It was a process which could be measured only over decades, and which continues today.

A case could be made, for example, that the public's esteem for Hollywood (in which Catholics were no different than anyone else) may have contributed to the contraceptive mentality. We reported above that Catholics were greatly in support of the Church's stand against birth control in the 1920's. However, there is evidence that this began to change with the Depression: one priest who worked in Phoenix in these years later attested that this was the sin most frequently mentioned in his confessional. Surely, the dire economic

straits of people in this time led a number of them to believe
that they could ill-afford more children—a mentality that only
arrived with people's near-total dependence on the indus-
trial-and money-economy for even their basic necessities.

Consider, though the images of male-female relation-
ships conveyed in the "classic" films of the period, and a
pattern clearly emerges: an "exciting" love affair in which
the principals pay attention only to their own feelings of the
moment, with only a superficial concern for marriage (or an
unrealistically "romantic" one), and even less of a concern
for a future family. One notices that there is usually no ac-
knowledgment of the fact that the "romantic" period is the
beginning of what should become, eventually, a holy family—instead, the clear message is that the *romance* is the thing
that matters, a message very conducive to the contraceptive
mentality.

One other important note about the Depression concerns a style of both architecture and interior decoration.
Old techniques, taste and style came in the 1920's to meet
new ones; it was considered that the world stood on the edge
of a new age, and so required a new look. Thus was born
Streamline Moderne, or as we call it today, Art Deco. At the
time it was seen as the coming thing, and everything from
glasses to churches (most notably the Shrine of the Little
Flower in Royal Oak, Michigan, and the Catholic Cathedral
in Salina, Kansas) were designed in it. Its original name gives
some impression of the style. Streamlined it certainly was.
Whether bric-a-brac or posters, things designed in this mode
gave the impression of straining either for speed or upward-
reach. There are two things to remember about Art Deco: 1)
it defined the 1930's; and 2) despite being thought of as
"Moderne," it was perhaps the last truly human style this
century. Where a procession can be seen from Romanesque
to Gothic to Renaissance to Baroque to Rococco and so on,

up to Art Deco, the line stops there, as the blaspheming, disordered, 20th Century would inevitably demand art of like character, especially after the unparalleled horror of the Second World War.

THE DEPRESSION UNDER HOOVER

The first reaction to the Crash was one of optimism. Throughout history, events have rarely been seen in their true light; so it was in this case. As Robert S. and Helen M. Lynd wrote of Middletown (actually, Muncie, Indiana), a typical Midwestern city, in their 1937 study, *Middletown in Transition:*

> Middletown entered 1930 prepared for the best. There had been a stock-market crash to be sure but...local bankers were predicting a boom in the spring...

> One of the most illuminating aspects of this early period of the depression was the reluctance of Middletown's habits of thought to accept the fact of "bad times." One does not like to admit that the techniques and institutions which one uses with seeming familiarity and control are really little-understood things capable of rising up and smiting one. The local press...became...a conscious and unconscious suppressor of unpleasant evidence. Hopeful statements by local bankers and industrialists...tended to make the front page, while shrinkages in plant forces and related unhappy news commanded small space on inside pages or were omitted entirely.

There were in fact a few spasmodic upswings in the economy in the months following the Crash which appeared to justify such optimism. But in May 1930, another downturn crushed such hopes.

It is a common myth to suppose that President Hoover did nothing in the face of the Depression. This widely-held notion (fostered afterwards by adherents of his successor) is ably summed up by Leo Gurko:

> Part of the country believed confusedly with President Hoover that the surest way to save the country was to imitate the techniques of the Puritan pioneers: reduce costs, tighten belts, close all the windows, bolt the shutters, and generally make oneself as small and inconspicuous a target as possible for the slings and arrows of misfortune. Politically, this took the form of cutting the budget, holding frequent conferences with the leaders of commerce and labor, issuing periodical statements that prosperity was just around the corner, declaring moratoria on foreign debts, praying, suggesting to factory owners that they not lower wages, and trusting that the system would get back on an even keel of its own volition. This program was attractive to a great many people because it involved them in the least possible effort and encouraged them to keep moving in familiar, hence more or less comfortable grooves (*The Angry Decade*, p.43).

So deeply held was this view that in the eyes of many, Hoover himself became personally responsible for the Depression. As it ground on, and millions were reduced to beggary, selling apples, and the like, the tent-and-shanty villages which the now-homeless constructed on the outskirts of major cities came to be called *Hoovervilles*. The same feeling was reflected in a popular song, whose best known line runs: *Mr. Herbert Hoover says now's the time to buy; so let's have another cup of coffee, and let's have another piece of pie!* But in fact, after time, Hoover began to fight the Depression strongly.

Although perhaps most people in 1930 thought that the American economy would pull through intact, a few voices were raised declaring that mere economic recovery was not enough; that a more thorough-going regeneration was in order. Two of the best-known groups of this sort had been saying the same things in the previous decade; but prosperity had severely limited their audiences. In hard times, as is ever the way in America, more were willing to listen.

The first group to enter the fray were the New Humanists, with the publication in February, 1930 of a group of essays entitled *Humanism and America: Essays on the Outlook of Modern Civilization*. Editor Norman Foerster opened his preface with the words:

> "Life's a long headache in a noisy street," sang the poet Masefield in *The Widow in the Bye Street* seventeen years ago. Since then we have all come to live in Main rather than Bye Street, and our headache has grown apace despite the best efforts of the physicians of the age. The noise and whirl increase, the disillusion and depression deepen, the nightmare of Futility stalks before us in the inevitable intervals when activity flags. Heroically or mock-heroically we distrust or reject such stimulants and anodynes as religion, moral conventions, the dignity of manners, the passion for beauty, and even our recent faith in democracy, in liberalism, in progress, in science, in efficiency, in machinery. At length revolt and skepticism themselves have ceased to be interesting. The modern temper has produced a terrible headache.
>
> In vain does our Chief Executive assure us that "we have reached a higher degree of comfort and security than ever existed before in the history of the world." Like Mr. Punch when it was announced that the government would soon be broadcasting intelligence by radio, we wonder "Where will the government get it?" All governments, all nations, are today in this predicament (p.v).

The fourteen following essays proposed rather similar

theories: that modern man had given himself up to his own whims, that he was urged by his opinion molders "to live as unconsciously and mechanically as possible," in the words of Gorham B. Munson (p.243). From this had resulted all our current problems. The answer, thought the New Humanists, lay in self-discipline, in reason, and in acceptance of "transcendent values." As noticed earlier, they disagreed (in a most gentlemanly manner) among themselves as to what these latter were, Irving Babbitt declaring for whatever spirituality was common to Christianity and to Buddhism; T.S. Eliot cleaving to external religious authority. To Babbitt, having commented on the joint Humanist and Catholic veneration for, say, Aristotle, "It follows that the Catholic and the non-Catholic should be able to co-operate on the humanistic level" (p.44). Eliot, however, had a rather more interesting view of the Church:

> The great merit of the Catholic Church, from the worldly point of view, is its Catholicity. That is to say, it is obvious that every religion is effectively limited by the racial characteristics of those who practice it, and that a strictly racial or national religion is certain to hold many irrelevances and impurities, from lack of an outside standard of criticism. When the Catholic Faith really is catholic, the aberrations of one race will be corrected by those of another. But it is obviously very difficult even for the Roman Church, nowadays, to be truly Catholic. The embarrassment of temporal powers, the virulence of racial and national enthusiasms, are enormous centrifugal forces. The great majority of English speaking people, or at least the vast majority of persons of British descent; half of France, half of Germany, the whole of Scandinavia, are outside of the Roman communion: that is to say, the Roman Church has lost some organic parts of the body of modern civilization. It is a recognition of this fact which makes some persons of British extraction hesitate to

embrace the Roman communion; and which makes them feel that those of their race who have embraced it have done so only by the surrender of some essential part of their inheritance and by cutting themselves off from their family (pp.106-107).

In all of this, there is much talk of the cultural and the spiritual, but little of the supernatural and the salvific. The New Humanists were severely hampered in dealing with the Church, as for them it was merely a generally positive force for cultural and spiritual values, rather than a supernatural one primarily concerned with their permanent union with God in the Beatific Vision, to which end a culture's values must ultimately be ordered. This is certainly in part due to the fact that their New England Yankee (whence most of them had sprung) heritage disposed them to think of the Church as something for other people; especially for one's Irish maids. But the greater responsibility lies with American Catholics. Men like the New Humanists knew the Catholic Church simply as the source of Gregorian Chant, Scholastic Philosophy, and Gothic Architecture. The fact that she sometimes also produces wonderful things in the artistic realm is secondary—both to the role she plays in sanctifying individuals, and the role she ought to play in creating a social order conducive to the promotion and maintenance of souls in the state of Sanctifying Grace. At any rate, because of this lack of realization of the Church's mission, the New Humanists could not realize her true place in the reconstruction of society or their obligation thereby.

The second drawback they faced was that they were literati and academics, not men of action. Hence they could produce no concrete program, or even a vision of the America they would like to see. Indeed, they scorned such as mere "legislationism." Their true sphere was criticism of the arts and education. But in a society such as ours, where such things are seen as being beyond the average individual's interests, their insights could have, ultimately, only a small audience.

All that having been said, however, it must also be pointed out that the New Humanists, if they were not offering real solutions, were at least asking questions which had not been asked; questions which, heretofore, *ought not* to be asked, at least not by true blue Americans. By their insistence that the life of the mind and spirit had a proper role to play in national life, they were defying the American religion. Given their antecedents, that was something.

More specific were the Southern Agrarians, most of whom had been part of the Fugitive Movement in the preceding decade. Twelve of them authored a joint manifesto entitled *I'll Take My Stand: The South and the Agrarian Tradition.* In many ways, it was a reply to *America and Humanism*:

> The "Humanists" are too abstract. Humanism, properly speaking, is not an abstract system, but a culture, the whole way in which we live, act, and feel. It is a kind of imaginatively balanced life lived out in a definite social tradition. And in the concrete, we believe that this, the genuine humanism, was rooted in the agrarian life of the older South and of other parts of the country that shared in such a tradition. It was not an abstract moral "check" derived from the classics—it was not soft material poured in from the top. It was deeply founded in the way of life itself—in its tables, chairs, portraits, festivals, laws, marriage customs. We cannot recover our native humanism by adopting some standard of taste that is critical enough to question the contemporary arts but not critical enough to question the social and economic life which is their ground (p.xliv).

Their basic contention was that the very things which the New Humanists decried were the product of industrial and banking civilization; further, that the South had resisted this to a greater degree than any other part of the nation, even despite its military defeat in the War Between the States. At long last, they believed, the South itself was succumbing. But if the country as a whole was ever to become a decent nation again, it would have to regain an agrarian culture. By this the Southerners (who included such men as Robert Penn Warren, Andrew Lytle, John Crowe Ransome, and later Catholic convert Allen Tate) meant not a pure farming society, "that has no use at all for industries, for professional vocations, for scholars and artists, and for the life of cities." Rather, it would be "one in which agriculture is the leading vocation, whether for wealth, for pleasure, or for prestige—a form of labor that is pursued with intelligence and leisure, and that becomes the model to which other forms approach as they may." Yet in this first collection, the Twelve themselves admitted that they had no practical means to bring about this necessary goal, only the conviction that it could and must be done.

If conservative intellectuals were considering such things, the Comintern in Moscow was doing so also. Like the New Humanists and Southern Agrarians, they believed in the need for thoroughgoing change; unlike them, they had a practical program for doing so. From 1930, Comintern ordered Communists around the world to penetrate the arts, the clergy, trade unions, and the like. Where formerly they had tried to build their own unions and declare themselves openly, henceforth they would practice a tactic called United Front. It is hard to realize since the fall of the Soviet Union, but Communism presented a real threat to American society. The Depression called forth, particularly among writers, artists, and actors, very many folk who saw in the rhetoric of the Communist Party a real solution to the horrible misery around them. In 1930, it was not so obvious that this misery

would be around for a while; but it became so as 1930 passed
into 1931.

The second full year of the Depression saw its destabiliz-
ing results around the world. In the Far East, the Japanese
government, whose population were on the brink of starva-
tion at the best of times, believed that only overseas expansion could relieve the pressure on them. One faction of government felt that this expansion should be aimed at Soviet
Siberia; another that the European colonies in Southeast Asia
were easier targets. But both areas would require consider-
able military strength. Manchuria, on the other hand, nomi-
nally linked to the weak Chinese government of Marshal
Chiang Kai-Shek, would be a more tempting target. An in-
cident was provoked, Manchuria invaded, and after Shanghai was occupied to force Chiang to negotiate, the war ended.
Manchuria became the Empire of Manchukuo, under the
last Chinese Emperor, although the country was of course
ruled by the Japanese.

Already, in the rest of the world, liberal democracies were
judged by many of their citizens to be incapable of either
staving off the Depression or the increased Communist threat.
Under Mussolini, Italy had been able, after a brief economic
downturn, to shrug off the Depression raging elsewhere. It
was thought that if traditional party politics could be sup-
pressed, and all a country's political and social forces mobi-
lized under a single leader, the Depression could be defeated.
In a pattern which would be repeated throughout the world,
Mussolini's skill in protecting his nation's economy was much
admired by Argentine general *Jose Felix Uriburu* (1868-
1932). It must be understood that Argentina at this time
was considered at once democratic and advanced; Buenos
Aires had well earned its nickname of "the Paris of South
America." The anti-clerical Radical Democratic Party had
held power since 1916. Seeing the helpless floundering of

the civilian government, Uriburu led an army coup against it in September of 1930. Installed as president in September, he abrogated his predecessor's labor legislation two months later. He then proceeded to remove Radical Democrats from national and state offices, and finally dissolved the National Assembly itself. Reformation of the constitution followed, decency and order were restored, and Catholic Action introduced. Uriburu then stepped down to allow for a presidential election. Although Argentina was far from removed from the Depression, its worst effects were muted.

In the other major South American nation, Brazil, the Depression had similar effects. On October 30, 1930, a military revolution ousted the civilian president and installed *Getulio Vargas* as president. Unlike Uriburu, but like Mussolini, Vargas had no real ideology of his own; rather, he cooperated with leftists and rightists alike, with anyone whose support would cement his power. Similarly, he was not a practicing Catholic like Uriburu, but knew how to speak to Catholics, like Mussolini. Eventually, he introduced the *Novo Estado*, the "New State," which like Mussolini's Fascist state, was essentially power, rather than ideology oriented.

As in Latin America, so too in Europe, the notion took root of mobilizing all national resources in the fight against the Depression. Germany saw Catholic Centre Party chief *Heinrich Bruening* become Chancellor. Assuming office on March 28, 1930, he increased taxation, reduced government expenditure, raised tariffs on agricultural imports, and cut salaries and pensions. When the Reichstag (Parliament) rejected much of his legislation, he persuaded President Paul von Hindenburg on July 16 to push it through using the emergency powers given him by the Constitution's article 48. Unwittingly, he had prepared the way for Hitler:

[Former Chancellor Hans] Luther who began it and

Bruening who repeated this stratagem were not evil men. The result of the precedent was all the more damaging for the very reason that Bruening was a man of unimpeachable integrity. He was doubtless the ablest German statesman of the whole period, save perhaps Stresemann, and even that exception many not stand. He was a man of singular probity of life, a devout Catholic, a deeply patriotic, patient, prudent, and courageous intellectual. He had devoted much of his life to editing and leading the Catholic Trade Union Movement in Germany. As Chancellor he lived with becoming modesty in a few rooms of the chancellery, using the public taxi instead of an imposing limousine, conducted himself with exacting frugality as an example of high citizenship in a period that called for high sacrifices from everyone, and gave numerous exhibitions of his purity and strength of character. He of course believed that he could save Germany from the danger that hung over her. (John T. Flynn, *As We Go Marching*, pp.144-145).

Ultimately, Bruening hoped to establish a Corporate State with a restored Monarchy; but, as will become apparent, Germany instead received a parody thereof.

In neighboring Poland, the government had been dominated since 1926 by Independence leader *Josef Pilsudski*. A fallen away Catholic, Pilsudski had ruled with the help of the Socialists. But under the stress of the Depression, Pilsudski and his left-wing allies parted company. In the summer of 1930, Pilsudski moved against his erst-while friends and established a rightist "Government of National Unity," which however left out the Catholic National Democrats.

The same desire for governmental unity became apparent even in Britain; not only was a mixed Conservative-Labor-Liberal National Cabinet established under Ramsay MacDonald, but similar regimes (like the South African "Fusion") took power elsewhere in the Empire. This was not considered enough in some quarters, however, and 1931, which saw both the formation of the National Government and Britain's leaving the gold standard (to conserve the precious substance) also saw the formation of the British Union of Fascists under *Sir Oswald Moseley*. The Depression also spurred interest on the part of British and Dominion people in Belloc and Chesterton's *Distributism*. This latter advocated the breaking up of large industrial and agricultural combines, and their replacement by many small holders. Colonel Douglas' *Social Credit*, with its advocacy of credit-free money distributed in large enough quantities to end deflation and bring both wages and prices up to an acceptable level, gained many adherents in both the British Empire and the United States.

As the first months of 1931 passed by with little financial relief in sight, Pius XI wrote an encyclical dealing with economic questions. Marking the anniversary of Leo XIII's *Rerum Novarum*, it bore the name *Quadragesimo Anno*—"Forty Years After." It comprised three major objectives: 1) to show the benefits brought by Leo's encyclical to the world at large and to the Church; 2) to defend that pope's social teaching and to develop it more fully; and 3) to examine the roots of the current social unrest, and to suggest a cure.

In addition to a reform in morality, and recognition of Christ the King, as he had recommended already in the 1926 *Quas Primas*, Pius called for wide distribution of ownership—even as did the Distributists. He went further to declare that the State must withdraw from many functions which it had usurped since the French and Industrial revolutions. Echoing Leo XIII, Pius decried the fact that:

> Things have come to such a pass that the highly developed social life which once flourished in a variety of prosperous institutions organically linked with each other, has been damaged and all but ruined, leaving thus virtu-

ally only institutions and the state.

To remedy this situation, the Pope called for the formation of vocational groups. Uniting both employers and labor in each given profession, they would be represented in some sort of governmental body, and have the highest amount of autonomy possible. It would be the job of the State to coordinate these bodies.

The ideas in this encyclical were suggested to the Pope in great degree by two German Jesuits: *Oswald von Nell-Breuning* and *Heinrich Pesch*. Having lived through the see-saw interwar history of Germany, and being grounded strongly in the German Catholic social tradition, the ideas here presented were called in their ecclesiastical form *Solidarism*. As might be guessed, the vocational groups resembled the guilds of English Guild Socialism, and the Corporations already being erected by Mussolini. But the Pope criticized these latter as being too State-dominated; rather than drawing their power from the grass-roots up, they appeared to be mere organs of governmental domination over each employee.

Interestingly, Solidarism, under that name, only found much favor among Russian emigres—specifically, the organization called NTS (National Union of Solidarists). As expressed by Walter Laqueur:

> Solidarism saw itself as the antithesis of the class struggle. Relations between classes were to be harmonious, with a strong state as supreme arbiter. This implied the rejection of both "excessive" liberal individualism and Western pluralism. There was to be freedom in the future Russia, but not unlimited freedom; nor did the NTS envision a multiparty capitalist system. Key industries were to be state-owned. Lastly, religion was to be of central importance in the future order, with the Orthodox church in a dominant position (*Black Hundred*, p.81)

Although, as Laqueur observes in the preceding paragraph, "This doctrine was by no means identical with the social teachings of the Catholic church which went by the same name," the divergence was primarily cultural rather than ideological.

The encyclical had the effect of galvanizing Catholics around the world in support of Distributist and Corporatist ideas. One such was Antonio Salazar of Portugal, who had become Prime Minister of that country in 1926. In 1932 he gave the nation a Corporative constitution. In this document, the ideas espoused by Pius XI were erected into law. The result was called (as in Brazil, although it was quite different from Vargas' Brazilian edition) the *Estado Novo*, the New State. Corporations representing labor and capital in every branch of industry were erected.

The economy of Portugal had been in foreign hands for a long time; Salazar restored the position of the Portuguese fishermen, farmers, and artisans. The Church reassumed her rightful place in the national life. He declared that when the country was ready, he would bring back her King. Above all, Salazar tried, as had La Tour du Pin, von Vogelsang, and the other Corporate theorists, to put an end to the rule of party and faction. In his own words:

> ...we seek to construct a social and corporative state corresponding exactly with the natural structure of society. The families, the parishes, the townships, the corporations, where all the citizens are to be found with their fundamental juridical liberties, are the organisms which make up the nation, and as such they ought to take a direct part in the constitution of the supreme bodies of the state. Here is an expression of the representative system that is more faithful than any other.

Another attempt to inaugurate a Catholic, Corporate state took place in Austria. The rump remaining from the Ger-

man-speaking areas of the former Empire was always in a
rather precarious position economically. The Depression hit
the country badly. The rise of the Nazis to power in Germany in 1933 caught the country in a vise; to stave off Hitler,
successive Austrian governments had to turn to Mussolini.
Moreover, the Socialists and Communists were very active.
Surrounded by dangers internal and external, Austrians
looked for strong Catholic leadership. They found it in *En-
gelbert Dollfuss.*

Born in 1892, Dollfuss had studied law and economics
at Vienna. He became secretary to the Lower Austrian Peas-
ant Federation, and in 1927 director of the Lower Austrian
chamber of agriculture. In 1931 he became chancellor. At
the Christian Social Party conference in April 1933, the need
to reconstruct Austrian society if it was to stave off its enemies was of paramount concern. At that conference, Dollfuss' assistant, Kurt von Schuschnigg declared that the "reconstruction of the state" was "indivisibly connected with
the reform of society," and that *Quadragesimo Anno* was the
guide. A new Corporative constitution was adopted on June
19, 1934.

It is a remarkable document. Its preamble reads: "In the
name of almighty God from Whom all justice emanates, the
Austrian people receives for its Christian, German Federal
State on a corporative foundation this constitution." In keeping with this, the concordat with the Holy See was elevated
to constitutional law. Corporative legislative bodies like the
Federal Cultural Council and the Federal Economic Council were erected. Dollfuss, lover of Austrian institutions that
he was, favored a Habsburg restoration. But although he
gave his county a good constitution, he did not see it in
operation for long.

The Austrian Nazis were fearful that Dollfuss' activities
would prevent the country's being annexed by Germany. On

July 25, 1934, a group of 150-200 Nazis seized the chancellery, and murdered Dollfuss. Although the attempted coup was put down, it was nevertheless a great blow to Austrian independence.

Dollfuss' constitution did survive him—for four years. At last, abandoned by the West, Austria submitted to her northern neighbor. For the short period that Dollfuss' reforms were in effect, they produced some excellent results.

Lithuania also attempted a similar solution to the problems of the Great Depression, Communism, and Nazism. After a pro-Communist government was deposed in 1926, Antanas Smetona, who had led the nation to independence in 1918, returned to power. Under his sponsorship, a new constitution in 1931 made Catholicism the religion of the State, and established Chambers of Commerce and Agriculture to function in typical corporative style. A 1935 law created a Chamber of Labor to safeguard the workers' cultural, economic, and social interests. Here again, only four years would pass before Soviet troops ended the experiment—but what was accomplished in the meantime showed great promise.

The next year, Lithuania's neighbor to the north, Latvia, adopted a Corporative government; this even though only 29% of Latvians were Catholic. Still, it conformed to the general pattern otherwise:

> A corporative form of government came into effect with the formation, in January 1936, of a National Economic Council, made up of the elected boards of the newly created chambers of commerce, industry, agriculture, artisans, and labor. A State Cultural Council was also created, consisting of the boards of the Chamber of Professions, and the Chamber of Literature and Art. These councils were allowed to collaborate with the respective government departments, individually and jointly. The

two National Councils constituted the Joint Economic
and Cultural State Council, which was convoked by the
President of the Republic, and worked in close collabo-
ration with the Cabinet of Ministers. The Joint State
Council represented all sections of the nation, including
the national minorities. It passed resolutions by a simple
majority vote of its members.

The reorganization of the producing population on a
guild basis was paralleled by a readjustment in munici-
pal and rural self-government, where elections were now
held along guild rather than political lines. A new com-
munal law provided for an organic coordination between
the various corporative chambers and the self-governing
territorial administrations. It was generally conceded at
the time that the direct participation of every producing
socio-economic group in the governmental machinery
insured that national unity which both public opinion
and the men in office sought as a remedy for the current
ills and a new foundation for the future security of the
state (Alfred Bilmanis, *A History of Latvia*, pp.360-361).

Needless to say, the Soviets put an end to all of that also
in 1940.

Quadragesimo Anno made such an impression in the
Netherlands that Corporations were actually formed at the
behest of the minority Catholic Party, and endowed with a
certain amount of governmental power in the 1938 constitution; World War II and German occupation ended this
experiment. In Belgium, Robert Poulet, a journalist, played
an important part in the *Réaction* group. This consisted of
men of letters, war veterans, corporatists, etc. Established in
1932, its organ for the next two years was the *Revue
Réactionnaire*. It tried to foster a "powerful current of opinion against parliament and democracy;" it felt that the old
parties must disappear and "abdicate their sovereignty into
the hands of the King." The King, who would govern with

the help of a corporatist system, would be given the most extensive powers, including legislation. In 1935 the *Revue Réactionnaire* was succeeded by the *Revue de l'Ordre Corporatif* (1935-1940) which continued the struggle for a "corporate monarchy." The previous year, Poulet and various other *Réaction* members took over the *Nation Belge*. This latter held that the parliamentary regime was dying, and should be replaced by a corporatist state organized around the King. Of similar views were Pierre Nothomb (b. 1887), writer and orator, founder of the weekly *L'Action Nationale* (1924-1930), and Paul Hoonaert, who was executed by the Nazis.

In Ireland, Corporatism inspired the work of Frs. Denis Fahey and Fr. E. Cahill; it also had some influence on the 1937 constitution. Quebec and Latin American nations outside Brazil and Argentina showed interest in the same ideas.

Beyond and alongside the guilds, corporations, or vocational groups ending class struggle, as envisaged by Pius XI, Catholics and others confronted by the Depression looked to certain other common motifs in reconstructing the social order. These included a strong national leader who would direct reforms: he might be the legitimate King, as advocated by the *Action Française*, the Belgians whom we have just mentioned, Dollfuss, and Chancellor Bruening—and as put into practice by Yugoslavia's Alexander and Bulgaria's Boris III; or else a purely self-made charismatic leader like Mussolini or Salazar. This leader would undertake the coordination of the nation's economic interests. National traditions would be the guiding ideology, and party strife would be removed or lessened. Above all, the country's financial system would be removed from the vagaries of international finance and run for domestic interests alone.

These basic ideas lent themselves to a dizzying multiplicity of interpretations, both from country to country and within each of them. Mussolini claimed to be a Corporatist, and his program had a certain resemblance to the Pope's. But the *Popolari* under Don Luigi Sturzo, his earliest opponents (and whom he managed, as we saw, to reduce in 1923) had as their motto, *Libertas*, a liberty which was not "the liberal, individualist, anti-organic atomic conception, which is based on the [false] conception of the sovereignty of the people." Similarly, in Germany, Bruening's support for the Corporate State was echoed by his Nazi enemies. What separated Sturzo and Bruening from Mussolini and Hitler was their belief that the executive should be a legitimate monarch, that the corporations should be directed from the bottom up, and that Catholicism, rather than the nation or race should be the defining element in social morality. With Hitler's advent to power in 1933, however, the strong attraction of a charismatic leader to a people made desperate by poverty and hungry for security at any price, became manifest.

Bruening had been unseated by a cabal of short-sighted politicians, who prevailed upon the aged von Hindenburg to dismiss him. His place was taken by the Catholic Franz von Papen; he in turn was replaced by General Kurt von Schleicher. At last, confident that they would be able to restrain Nazi excesses, Conservative leaders agreed to the appointment of Adolf Hitler to the Chancellorship. Von Papen became Vice Chancellor, but the old guard were woefully mistaken in their belief that they could control the Nazis.

Communist agitation and street battles between Reds and Nazis (to say nothing of economic hardship) had made the Germans think that security for freedom was a good bargain. When, on the night of February 27, 1933, the Reichstag building was set ablaze, it was suspected that the Communists had done it (to this day it remains unknown whether it was in fact started by them or by the Nazis). The next day, Hitler prevailed upon von Hindenburg to issue a decree "for the Protection of the People and the State." This had the effect of voiding constitutional protection for personal, property, and political rights. Although the Nazis failed to gain an outright majority at the March 5 national elections, Hitler persuaded the Reichstag to pass an Enabling Act which transferred legislative power to the cabinet. Shortly thereafter, the first concentration camps were built and given prisoners; Communists first, but others later.

As with the Fascists, the National Socialist movement was designed to be attractive to both Right and Left. The left wing of the party, under Ernst Röhm, began to press Hitler for radical social and economic changes and the abolition of the army. This began to worry both industrialists and military men, whose tacit support the regime required. The traditional Right felt threatened on grounds of freedom. In a Dresden speech delivered in July of 1933, von Papen declared:

> Who among us would have imagined it possible that within four months the National Socialists would have taken over the entire German Reich, that all the middle-class political parties would have disappeared, that our democratic institutions would have been eliminated as with one stroke of the pen, that the new chancellor would have assumed a degree of power that no German Emperor ever possessed.

Von Papen's concerns were borne out by Nazi actions over the following months. Ever more incidents of terrorism occurred, with Röhm's SA attacking opponents of the regime. But the wily Hitler used that time to ingratiate himself with von Hindenburg, by showing the old man that through the Nazi program of rearmament and voiding the Versailles treaty, Germany would again become a great nation. He further assured the highest leaders of the army and navy that he would muzzle the SA (the Storm Troopers or

Brownshirts) and make the German war machine something
to conjure with.

Von Papen, who had helped convince von Hindenburg
to appoint Hitler in the first place, began to seriously cast
about for some way to restrain the Nazis:

> By early June 1934 Papen had concluded that since
> Hitler was unwilling or unable to control his SA, he, the
> vice-chancellor, would have to move the government into
> action by calling public attention to the regime's mis-
> deeds. As a forum for this challenge, he chose the audi-
> torium of Marburg University, one of the few German
> universities that had shown any rel ictance to give the
> Nazi regime an intellectual stamp of approval. On June
> 17, before what he called "the intellectual aristocracy of
> Germany," Papen delivered a speech wi tten for him by
> the Christian Conservative intellectual Edgar Jung. Papen
> began by defending the Christian Conservatives' role in
> helping Hitler to power, explaining that the had hoped
> to "reform" the discredited Weimar democracy by "uni-
> fying" the divisive party system under the banner of
> National Socialism. They had meant this to be a "tem-
> porary" measure designed to clear the way for a creation
> of a "new spiritual and political elite." They had cer-
> tainly not intended to introduce an "unbridled dictator-
> ship" and a "revolution against order, law, and church."
> After cataloguing more precisely the ways in which the
> Nazis had violated fundamental values and institutions
> of "European civilization," Papen appealed to Hitler to
> distance himself from those of his followers who were
> "falsifying" his ideas. "No people," he warned, "can live
> in a condition of perpetual upheaval; perpetual dyna-
> mism can create nothing. Germany must not climb
> aboard a train traveling into the void, no one knowing
> where it might finally stop" (David Clay Large, *Between
> Two Fires*, pp.120-121).

Hitler was much disturbed by the favorable reaction this speech received. The result was the June 30 "Night of Long Knives." Leaders of the party's left wing like Röhm were killed. But the Right felt Hitler's wrath as well. Jung was murdered, as well as Erich Klausener, the German head of Catholic Action. The purge extended outside of Berlin. In Munich, old Gustav von Kahr, the Catholic Monarchist leader who had thwarted Hitler's 1923 putsch was hacked to death with axes; his body was then dumped into a swamp.

Yet, when it was all over, the army, reassured by the downfall of their SA rivals, ordered each soldier to take an oath of personal loyalty to Hitler. Hindenburg died; his presidential office was merged with that of Chancellor into the new post of *Fuehrer*–"Leader." Hitler's grasp on the country was complete.

But however uncomfortable his takeover, Hitler, through his public works (such as the construction of the *autobahns*) and rearmament programs, made good on his promise to lead Germany out of the Depression. Many Germans still distrusted and feared him. But as in Italy (and unlike Russia), so long as it produced economic results, regardless of whatever freedoms were lost, the majority would give the regime tacit support.

As will now become apparent, although subsequent events have led us to look at Hitler and Mussolini as simply evil men, and their peoples dupes, the Germans and Italians made a deal which was uncomfortably like that which Americans would soon make.

Although Hoover in the beginning of the Depression was little disposed to major action, his mood changed as the situation worsened. The country had tightened its belt to be sure; do-it-yourself shoe repair kits were all the rage among those who could still afford them. Dance marathons offered hard-earned money to those whose feet could survive the

strain. Agencies and private organizations gave relief, but it
began to run dry after three years of Depression. Since cities
and towns were going bankrupt, many could not afford to
feed the poverty-struck. Moreover, those who could do so
were withdrawing money–preferably in gold coin–and hoard-
ing it. In response, Hoover sponsored through Congress the
Reconstruction Finance Corporation, which lent 1.5 billion
dollars by the end of 1932 to help rebuild the devastated
economy. In May and June, 17,000 World War veterans arrived in Washington urging passage of a bill which would
allow them to cash their bonus certificates early. When the
Senate defeated the bill, the government offered the vets
money for their return trips to their homes; but the last 2,000
of the "Bonus Army" had to be driven out by troops led by
General Douglas McArthur.

At the 1932 Democratic Convention, Al Smith was defeated for the nomination by his successor as Governor of
New York State, *Franklin Delano Roosevelt*. "FDR," as he
was popularly called, was a product of what is considered
America's aristocracy. Cousin of Theodore Roosevelt (whose
niece, Eleanore, he married), he combined a refined and individual accent with the same impression of energy his cousin
had possessed. Charming, assertive, with a jauntily placed
cigarette holder seemingly hermetically attached to his teeth,
he radiated confidence. Well he might; having inherited from
outgoing Governor Smith a budget surplus of 15 million, he
would manage to leave the Albany Statehouse with a deficit
of 90 million. Despite this he was able to speak convincingly
of the need for radical economizing in government.

No matter. He fought the 1932 campaign against Hoover
on just this point, as well as demanding States' Rights. He
beat Hoover handily; his campaign song was the upbeat ditty,
Happy Days Are Here Again. Despite this, it would take a lot
more to quiet the loud chorus of *Brother Can You Spare a*

Dime?

In those days, since the inauguration took place on March 4, the outgoing president faced a four month long lame-duck period. In January, more and more banks failed. When, on February 14, 1933, the two largest banks in Detroit closed and Governor Comstock ordered a bank holiday for Michigan, Hoover decided that something similar must be done on a nation-wide basis, with the flow of gold out of the country being stopped as a corollary. As a lame-duck president, thoroughly discredited, who faced a Democratic congress, he did not feel able to carry out such a sweeping measure without the support of the President-Elect. He sent a note to Roosevelt on February 17 outlining the situation, asking him to do so publicly. Although FDR laughingly showed the note to friends, he did not reply to it. John T. Flynn tells the story:

> At the beginning of February, Hoover proposed to the Federal Reserve Board that every bank in the country should be closed for just one day. Each bank would then submit a list of its assets and liabilities. It would list its live assets and its dying or dead assets separately. The Federal Reserve would accept each bank's own statement. The next day all solvent banks would be opened and the government would declare them solvent and would guarantee their solvency during the crisis. That would stop the runs. As to the banks with large amounts of inactive assets, the live assets would be separated from the inactive ones. The banks would be reopened, each depositor getting a deposit account in proportion to his share of the active assets. The inactive assets would then be taken over to be liquidated in the interests of the depositors. This was an obviously sound and fair solution. Had it been done countless millions in deposits would have been saved and the banking crisis at least would have been removed from the picture. However, the Attorney-Gen-

eral ruled that the President did not possess the power to
issue such an order unless he could have the assurance of
Congress that it would confirm his action by an appropriate resolution, and that this, as a matter of political
necessity, would have to be approved by the new president who would take office in a month. It was some
such plan as this that Hoover had in mind when he wrote
Roosevelt on February 17. It had one defect from
Roosevelt's point of view. It would not do to allow Hoover
to be the instrument of stemming the crisis before
Roosevelt could do it (*The Roosevelt Myth*, p.22).

In accordance with this last, FDR refused to reply to
Hoover until they actually met on March 2, at which time
he refused to approve the plan. Although hundreds of millions in gold had flowed out of banks in the intervening
period, closing thousands of banks and businesses and sending unemployment through the roof, Roosevelt would not
act until he was inaugurated, and might take care of the
problem himself. In a manner of speaking, the bank crisis
would be Roosevelt's Reichstag fire. A nation desperate for
some solution would invest him with near total power, would
look to him as an economic savior.

MR. ROOSEVELT'S AMERICA
1932-1941

THE NEW DEAL

Roosevelt's inaugural address showed that he viewed himself as America's savior quite as much as did anyone else. After a great deal of lovely high-flown rhetoric, including the famous phrase, "the only thing we have to fear is, fear itself," he got down to brass tacks. If Congress failed to support his programs, "I shall not evade the clear course of duty that will then confront me. I shall ask the Congress for the one remaining instrument to meet the crisis—broad executive power to wage a war against the emergency as great as the power that would be given me if we were in fact invaded by a foreign foe....The people of the United States have asked for discipline and direction under leadership. They have made me the present instrument of their wishes." Of course, seeing that the Tenth Amendment to the US Constitution declares that "The Powers not delegated to the United States by the Constitution, nor prohibited to it by the States, are reserved to the States respectively, or to the people," one might wonder if even Congress had the right to invest such control in one man. But never mind. Roosevelt chose to take the fact of his election as a sort of Enabling Act.

Indeed, "The Hundred Days," as the period of time following his assumption of power were called, saw an unprecedented rush of legislation; after it passed, the old notion of governance in America had passed forever. At least Prohibition was ended; the newly legal alcohol had been seen as a possible source of tax moneys. When the 18th Amendment was repealed, the country went drunk with joy.

Once firmly in the saddle, Roosevelt convened an extraordinary session of Congress and ordered a bank holiday at last. In the same order, all trading in foreign exchange or transfer of credit abroad was forbidden under pain of fine or imprisonment—effectively confining to these shores anyone who might be tempted to leave with his money. On March 9, the Representatives and Senators gathered to consider a bill approving all that FDR had done. Unfortunately, the bill had not yet been prepared, so a folded newspaper was made to do duty until it was written up. Roosevelt then sent it on to the legislative branch who then passed it and gave the President full power over foreign exchange. The bill also authorized FDR to seize all gold held by individuals and corporations; failure to do so would result in a fine equal to twice the value of the gold held by the recalcitrant. Congress had signaled its willingness to join the Reichstag and the Italian Chamber of Deputies in becoming a rubber stamp.

April 5, 1933 saw the presidential decree requiring all gold to be turned in, adding to the authorized fine the threat of prison. This was an extraordinary event; residents of the alleged freest nation on earth would not be permitted to own (apart from jewelry or coin collections) gold. All gold coins would be withdrawn from circulation: the $20 Double Eagle, the $10 Eagle (in those days an "Eagle" was a basic currency unit, like the dollar and the cent), the $5 Half Eagle, and the $2.50 Quarter Eagle, all would go. Each gold dollar would be exchanged for its equivalent in paper money. Sold to the American populace as a purely temporary measure, it in fact remained illegal for Americans to own gold until 1974.

Had gold remained in private hands, the government's monopoly of banking and credit, its total control of the money supply, would have been challenged. As it was, the citizenry were told that their gold was being held in trust. Gold had been exchangeable always dollar for dollar, and would surely be so again when the emergency had passed. The Secretary of the Treasury, after all, had declared that "Those surrendering the gold of course receive an equivalent amount of other forms of currency and those other forms of currency may be used for obtaining gold in an equivalent amount when authorized for proper purposes." Nothing was said either about devaluing the dollar or going off the gold standard—had it been, the surrender of gold would probably not have been accomplished so easily.

In the meantime the treasury was empty. Treasury bonds were therefore issued, retaining the engraved promise of the United States Government to pay the interest and redeem the principal "in United States gold coin of the present value."

Then was passed, as a rider to the Emergency Farm Relief Act, the Inflation Amendment. This required the Federal Reserve Bank System to issue three billion dollars of Treasury Notes at the President's order, and gave him discretion to devalue the dollar by one-half. On June 5, Congress repudiated the gold redemption clause in all government obligations. Henceforth, the government would be able to redeem bonds or bank notes in whatever sort of money it chose. The same sort of clause in all private transactions was declared invalid. Then a new banking act gave the Federal government the power to tell banks how to lend their money, on what kinds of collateral; and in what proportions. Above all, under the act, banks might be cut off from the Federal Reserve System by government fiat: from the origin of the Federal Reserve to the act in question, the law read that the Federal Reserve Bank "shall" lend to a private bank on suitable security. This "shall" was amended to "may," thus making the transaction a privilege rather than a right, and giving FDR the effective power to strangle any bank he wished to.

Most interesting was Roosevelt's effort to force the dollar into inflation. Because the dollar was still quite strong, it did not fall in value when cut loose from gold by the inflation amendment. So, in FDR's words: "I am authorizing the Reconstruction Finance Corporation to buy newly mined gold in the United States at prices to be determined from time to time after consultation with the Secretary of the Treasury and the President. Whenever necessary to the end in view we shall also buy or sell gold in the world market. My aim in this step is to establish and maintain continuous control. This is a policy and not an expedient." From that time on, the government announced every day how much it would pay for gold: one day 30 paper dollars per ounce, the next 32, two days later 34. This meant of course that the value of the dollar fluctuated daily, and had the effect of halting loans; no bank could make a long term loan if it had no idea what the money with which it would be paid back would be worth. But the Soviet regime was strengthened by our purchases of Siberian gold.

FDR then put the government into the loan business in a big way. Through the Reconstruction Finance Corporation and the newly created Farm Credit Administration and Home Owners Loan Corporation, easy credit was extended to all. Since these bodies were not too concerned about being paid back, they could lend money on very easy terms indeed. Whence came the money for the loans? Apart from taxation, it came through the Inflation Amendment and an appropriation of $3,300,000,000 put into FDR's hands to fight the Depression any way he wished.

Next, on January 30, 1934, Congress passed a law giving the Federal government outright ownership of all the gold which folk had turned in, believing it would be returned. When Roosevelt asked Congress for the law, he declared that "I do not believe it desirable in the public interest that an exact value [of the dollar] be fixed." Nevertheless, the day after passage of the law, he did so, at 59% of its former gold value; the dollar was devalued by almost half.

But this was far from all that the New Deal encompassed. Roosevelt was a master of propaganda, insistently denouncing "the Old Order"—as in "We cannot go back to the Old Order." Symbolic as he made it out to be in his voluble radio "Fireside Chats," the dreadful Old Order had been nothing more than the three evil demons he conjured up: the "Economic Royalist," the "Brigand of the Skyscrapers," and most evocative of all, the "Modern Tory." A steady stream of anti-business propaganda was necessary if the next part of the New Deal was to succeed. This was nothing less than the complete subjection of every basic segment of the economy to Federal supervision.

One dilemma facing FDR was how to redistribute the national income. With control of banking and credit, he could do it; but in order to attach both the farmer and labor to his banner he had to avoid favoring one at the expense of the other. If he simply raised the farmer's income, labor would be annoyed. If he raised incomes equally, the farmer would not benefit. What, then, to do!

> The solution was a resort to subsidies. If the prices the farmer received were not enough to give him that share of the nation's income which he enjoyed before the world-wide depression of agriculture, the difference would

be made up to him in the form of cash subsidy payments out of the public treasury. The farmer on his part pledged himself to curtail production under the government's direction; it would tell him what to plant and how much. The penalty for not conforming was to be cut off from the stream of beautiful checks issuing from the United States Treasury. The procedure was said to be democratic. It is true that a majority of farmers did vote for it when polled by the Federal county agents. The subsidies were irresistible. More income for less work and no responsibility other than to plant and reap as the government said. Nevertheless, it led at once to compulsion, as in cotton, and it led everywhere to the compulsion of minorities (Garet Garrett, *The People's Pottage,* p.49).

Something similar was done with labor. By spending billions on employing young men in Federal labor projects, eight to ten millions of them were taken off the labor market, thus preserving the wage structure and the union monopoly of labor.

In addition to these measures, there came the establishment of the "Alphabet Soup" Agencies, so called from their acronyms. In toto, they covered every element of American life. Keystone of the system was the NRA, the National Recovery Administration. Established in June 1933, the NRA was to administer industry wide codes which would end unfair trade practices, reduce unemployment, establish minimum wages and hours and guarantee collective bargaining for labor. In the end, some 765 codes were established, governing the lives of 22,000,000 workers. Companies which accepted the codes displayed the blue eagle symbol of the NRA. The NRA had the effect of binding both larger companies, which application of its codes favored, and union leadership, to the New Deal.

The AAA (Agricultural Adjustment Administration) after its May 1933 debut administered the subsidy program;

the CCC (Civilian Conservation Corps) provided jobs for young men (18-25 years) in a paramilitary camp atmosphere. For a dollar a day plus roof and board they worked in the woods and fields, planting trees, stocking streams, protecting wildlife, and rebuilding historic sites. But of the many other agencies, the one which left the greatest tangible imprint on America was the WPA.

The Works Progress Administration, headed by *Harry Hopkins,* went to work on a number of tasks that formerly either local government or private donors would have provided before. A dizzying array of public buildings and roads, parks, playgrounds, and bridges sprang up all over the land. Many of them are still in use today (often in modified Art Deco).

But in addition to these sorts of projects, the WPA also funded artists in the Federal Art Project, which subsidized the decoration of hospitals, post offices, and schools–giving work to teachers, librarians, historians, draftsmen, and scientists; musicians in the Federal Music Project, which brought bands and symphonies to towns which had never enjoyed their benefits; actors in the Federal Theater Project, which put on performances of social protest plays; and the writers of the Federal Writers Project.

To this last came such great names as Conrad Aiken, Saul Bellow, Zora Neale Hurston and Lyle Saxon. Like many of the WPA projects, Communists were to be found in large numbers among its members, and hacks rubbed elbows with men and women of real talent. Set up on a state by state basis, the major work of the Project was the composition of the American Guide series–this latter offered guidebooks for each of the 48 states, Alaska, and Puerto Rico. Each was divided into three parts: the first would contain essays concerning general topics–natural setting, history, folklore, the arts, and so on; the second was always a profile of the major cities in the state; the last part would be description of the towns and villages to be seen on various automobile tours. Taken together with the added published material–regional guides, ethnic group descriptions, and so on, it must be said that the Project was able to portray America as it existed in all its rich diversity in 1938. In previous chapters we have incorporated material from these guides, which remain the most thoroughgoing survey of these United States ever attempted. In the words of project member Jerre Mangione:

> In addition to what they could do for themselves, the Project members, without realizing it, provided a powerful antithesis to the widespread obsession with proletarian writing that dominated the literary atmosphere of the thirties–the obsession which produced an outpouring of didactic writing that told and retold what was wrong with the country and what Marxist-Leninist solutions could save it from the evils of capitalism The project writers, during this same period, simply told their countrymen what their country was like. As Louis Filler put it, "...the Communist-minded writers could only talk about the bad time here and the good time coming, but the Federal writers could write about *their* country, *their* government: its present sorrows, weaknesses, and promise" (*The Dream and the Deal*, p.373)

In any case, the New Deal faced some legal challenges, no matter how much FDR might trample on the Constitution.

Congress had become a rubber stamp in the first year of the New Deal, and never regained its power while FDR was President. When it opposed him, it was severely denounced in the Press. Power, once given up, is never easily regained.

The Supreme Court at the beginning of Roosevelt's reign was chaired by Chief Justice Charles Evans Hughes. When the "gold cases," with their bait-and-switch treatment of the

American public and obvious governmental fraud came up, the Supreme Court ruled that what the government had done was immoral but not illegal; since the government had the sovereign power to commit an immoral act, it must be borne. But they ruled the NRA unconstitutional on May 31, 1935, thus arousing Roosevelt's ire at the destruction of one of his favorite programs. In 1936, the AAA was struck down. But on April 12, 1937, (after Roosevelt's re-election showed his popularity), the Wagner Labor Relations Act, making the Federal government the supreme judge of labor through the National Labor Relations Board was upheld. Chesly Manly's summation of this event may seem a trifle harsh:

> When the Supreme Court upheld the Wagner Labor Relations Act on April 12, 1937, the United States ceased to be a Republic with a government of limited powers, expressly enumerated in the Constitution, and became a welfare state on the European model, in which the national legislature has the power to regulate industry, agriculture, and virtually all the activities of the citizens. This concept of government was not completely established until the court upheld the Social Security Act on May 24, 1937, and the compulsory marketing quotas of the new AAA on April 17, 1939; but the New Deal principle of unfettered legislative authority was accepted when the court pronounced the Wagner Act constitutional. We still have the Bill of Rights, which safeguards the fundamental liberties of the people, but even this protection could be destroyed by treaties (*The Twenty Year Revolution*, pp.68-69).

In 1938 there was FDR's famous and unsuccessful attempt to pack the Court outright. In this he failed, but in time through death and replacement, he came to have a majority on the Court. From that time to this, the Court has rarely struck down Federal laws, preferring to interfere in

State and local affairs instead.

Although the States were immortalized as cultural and historical entities in the American Guides, Roosevelt relieved from them much of their remaining political identity. First, Roosevelt imposed Federal standards on the State social security systems, and made old age pensions and unemployment insurance a Federal thing. Then, huge grants in aid were made from the Federal Treasury to the States on condition they accepted Federal policies; since the citizenry clamored for what appealed to be free Federal money, it was a difficult offer to refuse. Thirdly, since the WPA, the Tennesee Valley Authority, and other such agencies were organized on a regional basis (the Writers' Project was a notable exception to this rule) State political and property rights were ignored. Fourthly, the Interstate Commerce Clause was extended into all sorts of areas not obviously under its sway.

Roosevelt's first term was conducted in a flagrantly unconstitutional manner, a fact not lost on his contemporaries, as the Supreme Court challenges make clear. But why, then, was there so little outcry? Caroline Bird provides an answer:

> There was something for everybody. For families, price supports. For the unemployed, Federal relief. For bank depositors, Federal insurance against bank failure. For investors who had bought worthless securities, Federal policing of security issuance and trading. Debtors took heart because the President was given power to inflate the currency, and mortgages were extended. Creditors were reassured by the pay and pension cuts. Business got protection from wage and price chiselers. Labor got protection for unions. In a crisis, mortgages could be stayed, gold impounded, banks closed, veterans deprived of their pensions and private parties of their property.

> No one really worried about whether all this was constitutional. Lawyers knew the powers were too vague to

stand up in court, but no one had the heart to push the point. When someone asked Fiorello LaGuardia, the dynamic representative from New York City, whether it was constitutional to prevent foreclosure of a mortgage, he pointed to my father, who was serving on a citizen's committee drafting a mortgage moratorium law, "Ask Mr. Bird, he's the lawyer here." Father and the other lawyers just laughed. The idea was to get something going and get it going fast (*The Invisible Scar,* pp.126-127).

Thus, in the end, Americans showed themselves quite as willing to barter freedom for security as either Germans or Italians. It is a sobering thought.

THE CHURCH AND THE DEPRESSION

Like the rest of America and the world, the Church was hard hit by the Depression. Church building ground to a halt for a few years, while the hierarchy concentrated on relief projects. *Quadragesimo Anno* prompted a huge outpouring of Catholic social thought and action around the world. In America, the Depression was seen as confirmation of the criticisms of capitalism contained in the Bishops' Program of 1919. In the intervening years, *Fr. Joseph Husslein, S.J.* and *Msgr. John Ryan*, among others, had worked hard to make the Church's view of society well-known, not merely among American non-Catholics, but Catholics as well (who are often just as ignorant of it). In this they were assisted by such Catholic journals as *The Commonweal.* But while, in America as abroad, almost all Catholics who knew of these teachings accepted them, they differed sharply on their concrete application. The result was that, in country after country, Catholics found themselves in conflict with one another; the cause was generally the nature of whatever non-Catholic allies this or that Catholic group had chosen to assist in accomplishing one or another of Pius XI's objectives.

In the beginning, the vast majority of Catholics (generally Democrats anyway) hailed FDR's assumption of power:

> Roosevelt presented to the nation what he called "a new deal," and for the most part the editors of *The Commonweal* were pleased with it. So were the great majority of Catholics and Catholic publications. Bishop Karl Alter of Toledo stated that the president's inaugural address "breathes the spirit of our Holy Father's recent encyclical." When speaking to Catholic audiences, Roosevelt himself referred to *Rerum Novarum* and *Quadragesimo Anno.* Richard Dana Skinner, drama critic for *The Commonweal* and an interested Democrat, wrote privately to party leaders that if Catholics "once understood clearly the identity of idea between the administration's efforts and the Pope's recent program of social justice, they would be more likely to give it enthusiastic support through thick and thin." Another staunch friend of the administration who was affiliated with *The Commonweal* was Father John A. Ryan, who had accepted an invitation to join *The Commonweal* editorial council in 1930. In later correspondence, Ryan would refer to Roosevelt as "the Miracle Worker in the White House" (Rodger Van Allen, *The Commonweal and American Catholicism,* p.43).

But as the New Deal continued, it became apparent to many Catholics that it was not all it was claimed to be. One of the first to dissent was none other than Al Smith. The Brown Derby had this caustic comment on the first year of FDR's reign: "Check the Constitution." Although originally a political ally of Roosevelt's, Smith would become one of his bitterest opponents.

On a level deeper than that of mere government, some Catholics began to realize that, beyond the obvious question of the Depression, America's ills required deep and spiritual solutions. A radical renovation of the nation's spirit would be necessary if there were to be any real change. One theorist of this sort was the French immigrant, *Peter Maurin.* Having come to this country in 1911, Maurin sought to spread the teachings of Leo XIII among the masses of people. In December of 1932, he met *Dorothy Day,* a former socialist convert, who had similar interest in bringing the Church to the Depression-struck. Although like her he wanted change, he hated what passed for much of social agitation at that time: "I did not like the idea of revolution...I did not like the French Revolution, nor the English Revolution. I did not wish to work to perpetuate the proletariat. I never became a member of a union, even though here in America I did all sorts of hard labor. I was always interested in the land and man's life on the land." In her forward to his *Easy Essays,* Dorothy Day describes his thought rather well:

> "People are just beginning to realize how deep-seated the evil is," he said soberly. "That is why we must be Catholic Radicals, we must get down to the roots. That is what radicalism is—the word means getting down to the roots."

> Peter, even in his practicality, tried to deal with problems in the Spirit of "the Prophets of Israel and the Fathers of the Church." He saw what the Industrial Revolution had done to the common man, and he did not think that unions and organizations, strikes for higher wages and shorter hours, were going to be the solution. "Strikes don't strike me," he used to say when we went out to a picket line to distribute literature during a strike. But he came with us to hand out the literature—leaflets which dealt with man's dignity and his need and right to associate himself with his fellows in trade unions, in credit unions, cooperatives, maternity guilds, etc.

He was interested in far more fundamental approaches. He liked the name "radical" and he had wanted the paper to be called *The Catholic Radical.* To him *Worker* smacked of class war. What he wanted was to instill in all, worker or scholar, a philosophy of poverty and a philosophy of work.

He was the layman always. I mean that he never preached, he taught. While decrying secularism, the separation of the material from the spiritual, his emphasis, as a layman, was on man's material needs, his need for work, food, clothing, and shelter. Though Peter went weekly to Confession and daily to Communion and spent an hour a day in the presence of the Blessed Sacrament, his study was of the material order around him. Though he lived in the city, he urged a return to the village economy, the study of the crafts and of agriculture. He was dealing with this world, in which God has placed us to work for a new heaven and a new earth wherein justice dwelleth. Peter's idea of justice was that of St. Thomas—to give each man what is his due.

The pair founded *The Catholic Worker* in New York, and the first issue appeared on May 1, 1933. Day's journalistic interests were in the social and industrial evils of the day—Maurin dwelled in his *Easy Essays* upon what ought to be done about them. His answer was threefold: Round Table Discussions, which would seek "clarification of thought" through discussion of the Church's teaching and its application; Houses of Hospitality, which would provide havens for the urban poor, and give them places to live, work, and discover the Faith in the midst of poverty—these would include soup kitchens and so on; and Farming Communities, where the same urban poor could be reintroduced to the land, and where a nucleus of a truly Catholic economy could be formed. Moreover, he advocated guilds. In addition to this, *The Catho-*

lic Worker opposed both usury and modern war. Their stance on the latter was motivated not by pacifism pure and simple, but by the belief that modern weapons made a "just war"—by the Church's standards—simply impossible. In all of this, there was nothing too groundbreaking in Catholic terms: Distributism, Guild Socialism, Social Credit, Solidarism, Corporatism—all had similar messages. What made *The Catholic Worker* unique was its desire to put these things in practice, not by capturing the organs of government, but by exposing the poor to them. As Maurin wrote in one of his quasi-poetic *Easy Essays*, (*op.cit.,* p.3):

> Writing about the Catholic Church,
> a radical writer says: "Rome will have to do more
> than to play a waiting game;
> she will have to use some of the dynamite
> inherent in her message."
> To blow the dynamite
> of a message is the only way
> to make the message dynamic.
>
> If the Catholic Church
> is not today
> the dominant social dynamic force,
> it is because Catholic scholars
> have failed to blow the dynamite
> of the Church.
> Catholic scholars
> have taken the dynamite
> of the Church,
> and wrapped it up
> in nice phraseology,
> placed it in an hermetic container
> and sat on the lid.
> It is about time to blow the lid off
> so the Catholic Church

may again become
the dominant social force.

In the years that followed, *The Catholic Worker* built up a network of hospitality houses in many of the nation's cities, as well as a number of farms. In subsequent wars in which this country was involved, they have inevitably protested (and been arrested for so doing) our involvement in them. Such work has brought them much into contact with radical leftist groups—thus leading many to consider them a left-wing group themselves. But in truth, although many times such associations have appeared to seem more important to various Catholic Worker members than their religion, this was certainly not the case with the founders; for that matter, in recent years their opposition to abortion has led to rifts with many whose company they had enjoyed on the barricades. After all, Maurin declared himself to be a man of the Right—but of course, he meant that in a European sense.

As at *The Catholic Worker*, so too at Baroness Catherine De Hueck's Friendship and Madonna Houses in Harlem, Toronto, Hamilton, Ontario, and elsewhere, it was considered that each poor person who came to the door should be given food and shelter as a right, not as a privilege. The Baroness moreover cultivated a special apostolate toward Harlem's blacks, to show them that real liberation would be theirs only through the Truth of the Catholic Faith. Both *The Catholic Worker* and Friendship House did not believe in just filling the mouth of the hungry, nor yet in spreading the Faith alone. Rather they tried to educate those who came to them in the Church's social teaching. In his *Easy Essays*, as in his conversation and lectures, Maurin revealed to the poor the teachings of such as Chesterton and Belloc, Alphonse Lugan, Eric Gill, Southern Agrarian Andrew Lytle, Gothic Architect Ralph Adams Cram, Economist R. H. Tawney, Guild Socialist Arthur Penty, and many others. The response of the poor was enthusiastic. Baroness De Hueck had a similar experience:

> The door of Toronto's Friendship House library opened with a bang and three men walked in. Two were still in their working clothes, their faces smeared with coal dust. They were engineers in a nearby factory. The third looked tired and thin, and his clothes bore the obvious stamp of city relief supplies.
>
> They called out a cheery "Good-afternoon" and asked if any new copies of their favorite magazines had come. By "their favorites" these particular three meant *The Commonweal, The Sign, America,* and *The Catholic Worker.* Some new copies had just arrived and the three settled down to enjoy them. An hour or so later, they announced they had to go. Before they went, they asked to borrow some books.
>
> With the card index file before me, I marked off the volumes just returned. Christopher Hollis, *The Breakdown of Money,* was the first. I noticed with gratification that it had been out four hundred times in the last year. Arnold Lunn's *Now I See,* was next. It had been out three hundred and seventy-five times. Fanfalli's *Catholicism, Protestantism, and Capitalism* was the third. It had been out three hundred and forty-two times. Naturally, we had several copies of each.
>
> Before I had time to ponder further on the significance of the popularity of this type of writer, my three friends had made their selection. Again as I checked I felt there was much food for thought. For before me lay *Selected Papal Encyclicals,* Dawson's *Religion and the Modern State,* and Berdyaev's *The End of Our Times* (Baroness Catherine De Hueck, *Friendship House,* pp.17-18).

With the apparent collapse of the American system, there was a hunger in the land for a replacement—hence the easy acceptance of the New Deal. But the New Deal could not alter the fact that something was hollow in the country's heart. That something was the lack of the Catholic Faith. Where *The Catholic Worker*, Friendship House, and similar apostolates tried to work on individual souls in hopes of changing the country in the long run, others attempted quick projects. Hence Msgr. Ryan, dubbed "The Right Reverend New Dealer," attempted to baptize Roosevelt's programs simply by saying they were in accord with Papal teaching, and then by defending them against all comers.

In a more constructive vein, the National Catholic Rural Life Conference, founded at the behest of the bishops in 1923, extended its work in the face of the Depression eleven years later. This operated to help the Catholic farm population retain its position in the face of the economic disaster, and to assist Catholic urbanites in resettling on the farm.

These and many other efforts made some local impact. But the one Catholic voice heard most loudly throughout the dark years of the Depression was the cultivated tone of Canadian-born *Fr. Charles E. Coughlin,* pastor of the Shrine of the Little Flower in Royal Oak, Michigan, outside Detroit.

Fr. Coughlin had in 1926 been assigned Royal Oak in the face of dominance of the town by the Ku Klux Klan. They burned down the church he built; as he stood over the charred embers, he looked skyward, and vowed that he would build a church "with a cross so high...that neither man nor beast can tear it down." He did so. But to raise public knowledge about the Church, and to fight bigotry, he took to the radio airwaves, making his first broadcast on October 17, 1926. For the succeeding three years, he kept to doctrinal themes, with occasional blasts against birth control (just then becoming popular) and the Klan. But on January 12, 1930, he addressed politics for the first time, denouncing Communism.

Coughlin had always had a great love of the poor, and had been a member of the Basilians, an order dedicated to social work. The Archbishop of Detroit, Michael J. Gallagher, had moreover studied in Austria during the 1890's, when Leo XIII's teachings were first enunciated. The Depression having broken out, nothing pleased the Archbishop more than the idea of having the social teachings on the air.

In his broadcasts, Fr. Coughlin reiterated the fact that Capitalism had bred the conditions necessary for the growth of Communism. He declared in the fall of 1930, "The thoughtful American is now convinced that the most dangerous communist is the wolf in sheep's clothing of conservatism who is bent upon preserving the policies of greed, of oppression and of Christlessness." In all his speeches, Fr. Coughlin assured his audiences that the beliefs of Christ and the Founding Fathers were the same; when he spoke of the Cross or the Saints, the Flag and Washington and Lincoln were never far behind. Like most Catholics in the US, he was an Americanist—the more so, perhaps, because he was an immigrant. In any case, he always avoided proselytization and indeed came out for religious liberty.

In any case, he met FDR in 1932, and became his staunch supporter. During the election he coined the catchy phrase, "Roosevelt or Ruin." Certainly, with his by then national radio audience, the Detroit priest was a figure to be cultivated by the new President.

Throughout 1933, the radio priest urged the remonetization of silver as an alternative to the now absent gold. Although FDR declared his appreciation of Coughlin's advice, he followed none of it. For his part, Fr. Coughlin began to find the behavior of the Alphabet soup agencies— the subsidies for crop destruction by the AAA and the monopolization encouraged by the NRA, for example—distasteful. Although still protesting his loyalty to FDR, he began to let drop such statements as, "I am for *a* New Deal." On November 11, 1934, he started the National Union for Social Justice, whose preamble and principles may be read in Appendix I. While it is obvious that point one contradicts Pius IX's *Syllabus of Errors*, points six, seven, and eight put Fr. Coughlin and the National Union on a collision course with Roosevelt. For while FDR had captured control of the country's credit and banking, it had not been for the sake of the population; indeed, the powers of the Federal Reserve had been immeasurably strengthened by New Deal measures.

The open break with FDR came over the proposed entrance of the United States into the World Court, a proposal favored by the administration. Senate debate on the treaty came to an end on Friday, January 25, 1935. On Sunday, Fr. Coughlin delivered a stinging attack on the notion, declaring that it would end American sovereignty and put the country under the thumb of international financiers. He urged his audience to flood Washington with telegrams; they did so. Over 200,000 telegrams featuring one million names came into Senatorial offices. The measure was defeated, and FDR, who had staked much personal prestige upon this treaty, was heavily stung.

The rift was unbridgeable. Fr. Coughlin would, with such men as *Fr. Edward Lodge Curran* of Brooklyn, (head of the Catholic Truth Society there), eventually organize the Christian Front, which would be a source of opposition to administration policies until the beginning of World War II. To the same end would be turned his newspaper, *Social Justice*. But Fr. Coughlin's greatest battle with FDR would already have been fought by then; the election of 1936, which he would wage with the aid of non-Catholic allies. After that he would make common cause with right-wing groups of more or less respectability. In a word, he became a mirror image of *The*

Catholic Worker's leftist trend.

What strikes the observer, decades later, was the reluctance of either the official hierarchy (represented by such as Msgr. Ryan) in their zeal for the New Deal, Fr. Coughlin and his connection with certain right-wing factions, or *The Catholic Worker* with their socialist allies, to break entirely free of the Americanist trap. Based upon common compartmentalizing ideology, they still would not see the need for an effort to convert the nation to the *authentic* Christian religion. Instead they tended to take the easy way out of purely or mainly political activity, accepting uncritically the notion that the American civic religion was somehow Christian and compatible with Catholicism. Only Peter Maurin warned that "Christian Democracy is not possible without Christian Aristocracy." But his criticisms would be echoed primarily outside Catholic circles.

OPPONENTS OF THE NEW DEAL

If most Catholics happily accepted the New Deal immediately, many other folk did not. The first active source of opposition to FDR was a group of industrial and financial magnates (including J.P. Morgan, the Du Ponts, Andrew Mellon, and General Motors) who organized in September 1934 the American Liberty League. Al Smith was a prominent member of it, and it included a great many folk who feared that the New Deal was simply Socialism under another name. At one point, its leaders even contemplated a military coup against FDR. But when, after the election of 1936, its big business sponsors decided to make peace with Roosevelt, the American Liberty League was disbanded by them. Their opposition to Roosevelt was not ideological at all, but purely fiscal. Their piece of the pie assured, their enmity vanished.

The opposition of others to the New Deal was rather more serious. In April of 1933, Seward Collins, editor of *The Bookman,* a journal primarily influenced by the New Humanists (Collins was a disciple of Babbitt in the beginning) replaced it with a new periodical, *The American Review.* In his opening editorial, he stated:

> The *American Review* is founded to give greater currency to the ideas of a number of groups and individuals who are radically critical of conditions prevalent in the modern world, but launch their criticism from a "traditionalist" basis: from the basis of a firm grasp on the immense body of experience accumulated by men in the past, and the insight which this knowledge affords. The magazine is a response to the widespread and growing feeling that the forces and principles which have produced the modern chaos are incapable of yielding any solution; that the only hope is a return to fundamentals and tested principles which have been largely pushed aside. Fortunately, there is no lack of able men to represent this traditionalist point of view, although they have been forced to work in isolation from each other and have achieved nothing like the influence to which their stature entitles them. It should be obvious that a periodical aiming to bring these groups and individuals together is particularly needed in this country, where tradition took little root before it was overridden by the disruptive forces that are now threatening Western civilization. In Europe the spokesmen for sanity and order are more numerous and more solidly entrenched: they have built up such a weighty mass of indictment and prescription that they can be said to have their modernist foes already on the defensive. For this reason we shall frequently be drawing on European contributors, but the editorial emphasis will be directed to the needs of this country.

He went on to describe some of the groups that would find a voice in his magazine. The New Humanists would find their niche, of course. But the Distributists would also be represented, and in fact both Chesterton and Belloc contributed to this and subsequent issues. In this way they were introduced for the first time to the non-Catholic American public. Then too, the Southern Agrarians were present also, as were the Neo-scholastics, those folk who repopularized St. Thomas Aquinas. T.S. Eliot, Christopher Dawson, Charles Maurras, Henri Massis, and various other Europeans of like mind would also add their input. In a word, Collins hoped to produce a "forum for the views of these 'Radicals of the Right' or 'Revolutionary Conservatives.'"

As the journal developed in the years of its life from 1933 to 1937, all these views and many more—Monarchist, Corporatist, Guild Socialist, and so on, were encountered in an American context. One eminent writer brought to public view by the Review was *Ross J.S. Hoffman,* a convert. His essays in Collins' magazine were published in 1935 as *The Will To Freedom;* his 1938 *Tradition and Progress* and 1939 *Organic State* elaborated the Catholic view of social reform.

Above all, *The American Review* brought together these varied folk in a way that would have been impossible without it. One product of this conjunction was the publication of a volume two years before *The American Review's* demise, *Who Owns America?* Subtitled "A Second Declaration of Independence," it was edited by Herbert Agar and Allen Tate. Although conceived of as a sequel to *I'll Take My Stand,* it offered in addition to the Southern Agrarian writers the Ohioan Willis Fisher, who argued for the integrity of non-Southern regions against the ever centralizing state; Hilaire Belloc, who of course put forward the Catholic and Distributist view; and Douglas Jerrold, Catholic editor of *The English Review,* who would the next year fly General

Franco from the Canary Islands to Spanish Morocco in his private plane (thus doing his part in the Spanish Civil War). As Agar wrote in his introduction:

> Among the authors of this book there are Protestants, agnostics, Catholics, Southerners, Northerners, men of the cities and men who live on the land. There are two Englishmen, who give the European background of the problems which afflict our country. Our common ground is a belief that monopoly capitalism is evil and self-destructive, and that it is possible, while preserving private ownership, to build a true democracy in which men would be better off both morally and physically, more likely to attain that inner peace which is the fruit of a good life (p.ix).

Like its predecessor, and like the journal in which many of its authors encountered each other for the first time, *Who Owns America?* offered a cogent critique of both the New Deal and the American system which spawned it. But all these protests were (despite their inherent value simply in being uttered) ultimately of no effect. Certainly, FDR lost no sleep over them, any more than he did over the fulminations of the Technocrats (who wished to beat the Depression by turning control of the country over to scientists, who they thought could best figure out something so complex), or Upton Sinclair's EPIC (End Poverty In California) movement, which would have established the Golden State as a vaguely Socialist entity. None of these folk came remotely close to achieving power in any area of the country. The only individual who offered a real challenge to the New Deal was "the Bonaparte of the Bayous," *Huey Long* of Louisiana.

Elected Governor of Louisiana in 1928 as a Populist opponent of big business, Long soon had the entire state completely under his thumb. He ran Louisiana more like a Latin American dictatorship than like a state. But while in office he made many improvements, particularly in roads and education. The result was that to this day people in the Creole State are severely divided over him.

But there were similar folk elsewhere in the country who ran states or regions more or less like benevolent despots. Frank Hague, mayor of Jersey City, dominated the whole of New Jersey with the support of local Catholic organizations like the Knights of Columbus; Mayor James Curley of Boston; Governor Eugene Talmadge of Georgia, Governor Bibb Graves of Alabama, and many others fit the bill. In a time when the Depression-wracked populace were looking for economic salvation, the same impulse which had brought FDR to power was at work on the state and local level, and had similar results.

What set Long apart was his ability to project an ideology, and to become a national figure. It would have been impossible to think of Hague or Talmadge as President; by 1935, it was not impossible to think that way of Long.

Having broken all opposition in Louisiana, Long was able to secure a puppet's election as governor in 1930, and in that year went to the Senate in Washington (although when at home in Baton Rouge he would still conduct sessions of the state legislature). The next year he was able to procure the election of an ally as Senator from Arkansas; it was a first sign of his influence beyond state boundaries. He used that influence to help win first the nomination and then the election of 1932 for Franklin Delano Roosevelt.

But Roosevelt soon tired of Long as he had of Fr. Coughlin. The rift took place in 1933. Long took to the airwaves as Fr. Coughlin had, and like the radio priest soon built up a national movement. This was centered upon his "Share Our Wealth" plan, first enunciated in his autobiography, *Every Man a King*. The basis of it was the limiting of all incomes to one million dollars a year, the remainder to be given to the government and distributed among the rest of the populace. It was a program which, while not directly threatening class warfare, was revolutionary enough to make the wealthy fearful and the poor hungry. By 1935, Long was beginning to look like a real threat to FDR in the election to be held the next year. He insouciantly published a "novel," *My First Days in the White House,* describing the beginning of a Long presidency (in which he magnanimously gives a cabinet seat to his defeated predecessor, FDR).

Fr. Coughlin, in the meantime, began to look forward to allying his supporters with Long's; this grouping would be completed by the adherence of Dr. Townsend, a social theorist who advocated a revolving pension for old people; they would be required to spend all the money they thus received—the economy would be stimulated and their lives bettered. This threeway conjunction appeared to have a chance of propelling Long right into the White House.

Luckily for Roosevelt, this possibility was stilled by an assassin's bullet on September 7, 1935. Dr. Carl Weiss, the murderer, was killed immediately by Long's guards at the Statehouse where the shooting occurred. The perpetrator dead, rumors of outside conspiracies abounded; to this day in the bayous and small towns of Louisiana, some whisper that FDR, "mus' a' had sompin' to do wid it." Whether or not that is so (and political assassinations with dead assassins are always fonts of conspiracy theories) this was not a death Roosevelt could have been too hurt by.

With Long dead, his machine turned inward, toward retaining their grip on Louisiana (which they managed successfully to do, thus staving off Federal corruption charges which would have sent many of them off to jail had they not agreed to end all activities outside their own state). Long's national organization, presided over by one Gerald L.K. Smith, was thus cut off from its base of support and left to fend for itself. Nonetheless, Smith, Townsend, and Fr.

Coughlin decided to go ahead as planned. They formed the Union Party in May of 1936, and nominated Representative William Lemke of North Dakota as their Presidential candidate. The three backers prepared to fight the election.

Fight it they did, as did the Republican nominee, Alf Landon of Kansas. But the Union Party, bereft as it was of the charismatic Long, for all the letter writing and radio broadcasting received only 892,378 out of 45 million votes—less than two percent. Despite the support of the Liberty League and stalwart campaigning on his behalf by Al Smith, Landon did worse than any major candidate had up to that time; failing to carry even his native Kansas, he had to be content with just Maine and Vermont. Up to that time, Maine had been a bellweather of elections, consistently electing the victor; hence the then prevalent saying, "As Maine goes, so goes the nation." Roosevelt triumphantly quipped, "As Maine goes, so goes Vermont."

Triumphant FDR well might be. With the thrashing of all his foes at the polls, there was now no significant challenge to him; he was at last in complete control. Fr. Coughlin and the tattered remnants of various movements remained, but they were no threat. He yet had one major problem, however. For all the rhetoric and posturing and New Deal legislation and sound and fury, the Depression, despite occasional flurries of prosperity, still retained its icy grip upon the land. If he was to retain power, he must somehow break that grip. Luckily for him, hope—in the form of war clouds—was on the horizon.

COUNTDOWN TO WAR

In the great world outside, things were indeed going from bad to worse. The Far East saw the continued attempts by both Japan and the Soviet Union to dominate ever more of

China. While Manchukuo was being formed into a Japanese puppet state, the Soviets were completing similar work with Outer Mongolia. The Japanese, who as earlier noted felt compelled to dominate China for economic reasons, were now forced to redouble their efforts in the northern part of the country to stave off the Soviets. On November 16, 1933, FDR recognized the Soviet Union; the policy of non-recognition was applied to Manchukuo, and the impression given Japan that while Soviet colonization of China was all right, Japanese was not. After all attempt at renewing the traditional US Japanese alliance failed in 1934, Tokyo began to draw close to the new regime in Berlin.

Meanwhile, Germany reoccupied the Rhineland and Italy seized Ethiopia in the year of 1936. American response to the latter was to apply sanctions and hold aloof from any negotiation. But the big event of the year was the outbreak of the Spanish Civil War.

After Alfonso XIII had been forced out of Spain in 1931, a parliamentary republic established in his exile tottered ever leftward. Violence against Catholics and Conservatives rose, and by mid-1936 it became apparent that either the Right-wing army or the Communist militias would revolt; the army struck first. General Francisco Franco was flown from his command in the Canary Islands to Spanish Morocco by Douglas Jerrold. There he raised the standard of revolt, led his troops into the Spanish mainland, and began a three year conflict which would end with the extinction of the progressively more Communist Republic.

The Falange, one of several political factions within Franco's national coalition maintained the following point along with the 27 others in their program:

> 25. Our movement incarnates a Catholic sense of life—
> the glorious and predominant tradition in Spain—and shall

incorporate it into national reconstruction. The Clergy and the State shall work together in harmony without either one invading the other's domain in such a way that it may bring about discord or be detrimental to the national dignity and integrity.

The others dealt with the regeneration of Spain and the establishment of a Corporate State.

Given this sort of ideology, the two sides soon attracted foreign volunteers. France, Britain, and the US followed a policy of "non-intervention" which meant that they would not sell arms to the "Loyalists," as the Republican government's adherents were called; the Soviets armed them, and foreign leftists flocked to their banners. Germany and Italy sent troops, and several thousand Portuguese joined Franco's ranks. But the conflict was a world war in miniature. Two brigades of Americans—the Abraham Lincoln and the George Washington—fought with the Loyalists, as did such luminaries as later Bulgarian dictator Dimitroff. On the Nationalist side, in addition to the three nations named, six hundred Irish "Blue-shirts" under General Eoin O'Duffy served, as did a number of others. About 1,000 foreigners of other nationalities served with Franco in the winter of 1937-1938. These included some French *Camelots du Roi,* White Russians, Latin Americans, Romanian Iron Guardists, a handful of English, Canadians, and Americans, and a few interesting characters like South African Catholic poet, *Roy Campbell.*

The victory of the Nationalists was a Godsend to like-minded folk throughout Latin America and elsewhere; but the tacit support of the Loyalists by Roosevelt, as well as the continued support by our government for anti-clerical groups and regimes were not forgotten. At a time when Catholic Spain seemed again a strong nation, her descendants in South America rallied to her. In Colombia, *Laureano Gomez,* leader of the Conservative Party, provided a focus of Catholic and Hispanic loyalty, as this quote from a Colombian paper of the time shows:

> We were born Spanish....We speak the tongue of Castile because we can speak no other....The twenty cowardly governments of Latin America have put themselves into the hands of foreign nations, dedicated to false liberalism and to Masonic, atheistic democracy....The panorama is desolate...we are still conquered territory...

> *Hispanoamerica,* the land of vassalage...Each day the yoke of Saxo-Americana is drawn tighter around our throats. Sometimes the yoke is of steel, sometimes of silk, soft and perfidious...

> But–all is not lost. There is still heard the voice of Laureano Gomez to tell the truth about the future, to direct us to the road of tomorrow, the Catholic Hispanic Empire.

> *And we will go back to Spain.* The five arrows of Ferdinand and Isabella, the symbol of Catholic unity, will be our symbol also. It is written in the future of America by the inscrutable hand of Providence.

In Ecuador was a similar group led by Jacinto Jijon y Caamaño. In Lima, Peru such opinions were expressed by the newspaper *El Comercio,* and its owner Carlos Miro Quesada Laos. Havana boasted the paper *Diario de la Marina,* whose editor Jose Ignacio Rivera continued the Carlist traditions of his family. Even in the American-held Philippines, a branch of the Falange existed, organized by Andres Soriano and Enrique Zobel. Puerto Rico had a similar organization.

But most interesting of all were the Mexican Sinarquistas. Wanting to set up a Catholic Corporate state in Mexico, the

April, 1939 issue of their journal, *El Sinarquista,* declared:

> All those who have been concerned with dignifying the life of Mexico, as well as those who have wanted to point the way to the real aggrandizement of Mexico, speak of Spain. To put it more concretely, they speak of the work done by the Mother Country during the historical colonial period. She showed us the road and gave us our bearings. So Mexico must cling to its traditions to find the meaning of its future. Thus, those who feel the desperate uncertainty that today hangs dense and heavy over the nation, want to return to Spain.

By 1941 they were well established throughout Southern California and South Texas, thus giving more than abstract interest to Fr. Coughlin's observation in *Social Justice*: "Advocates of Christian social justice in America, Christian Americans who once dreamed of a national Union to effect a 16-point reform, and who have watched the progress of the Christian states headed by Salazar, De Valera, General Franco..., will want to hear further from Mexico's Sinarchists with their '16 principles' of social justice." But in truth, there could be no triumph of Catholic principles in Latin America without a similar triumph in Europe; Spain, Ireland, Portugal, and Poland put together would not be enough to shield our southern neighbors from the US government's habitual pressure. Who then could they turn to in Europe? Not Britain and France, who were, in any case, weak and distracted. That left only Germany and Italy, who, as a result of the Ethiopian sanctions, were drawing closer to one another. Many a Latin American Conservative thus made the mistake of turning pro-Axis.

Meanwhile, collusion between Hitler and Mussolini led to the snuffing out of Austria, and its absorption by Germany. This led to the encircling of Czechoslovakia by the Reich, and the Munich crisis. On August 18, 1938, FDR gave a speech at Queen's University, Kingston, Ontario, in which he declared that the Monroe Doctrine covered Canada, and by extension, the entire British Empire. This was taken by the French and British as a pledge of alliance should war break out. However, the menace was averted by the famous appeasement of Munich, and so Roosevelt would have to wait for events to develop in his favor. Unfortunately, the economy, which had been stable, took another dive.

The Sudetenland having been absorbed, Hitler shocked Europe by his takeover of Prague and the remaining Czech lands on March 15, 1939; Slovakia became independent under Msgr. Tiso, and Ruthenia did so likewise, preparatory to being absorbed by Hungary.

Outright war had broken out between Japan and China in 1937. Rapidly the Japanese had seized Shanghai, Peking, and the capital at Nanking. Chiang Kai-Shek was forced to retreat into the country's interior, and to rely heavily on the Communist guerrillas who had been his longtime foes (and would be again). On October 5, the President gave a speech in Chicago, abandoning his policy of taking no sides in the conflict and suggesting a need for economic sanctions against Japan. Apparently an economic downturn and the revelation that newly appointed Supreme Court Justice Hugo Black was a former Klansman required a speech that would get everyone's mind off troubles at home. While a large bloc of newspapers supported the President's new stand, the Catholic Press did not. The Jesuit *America* stated (October 16, 1937), the "people of the United States are positively opposed to any foreign imbroglios."

While that was certainly true, it did not effect FDR's conduct. Time after time, in the remaining years leading up to Munich, peace feelers and initiatives sent out by both Germany and Japan were brazenly rejected. It might be objected to this point that both regimes were already guilty of oppressive behavior; however, as noted, Roosevelt had done his best to cultivate friendly relations with the Soviet Union, which under Stalin had carried out yet another bloody purge in 1936. Surely, then, what could little things like atrocities mean to us?

When war broke out between the British and French on the one hand, and the Germans on the other over the latter's invasion of Poland, Roosevelt, as was customary, invoked our neutrality. Almost as soon as he had done it, though, he began to circumvent it. On September 2, 1940, the famous "Destroyers for Bases" deal was concluded between Britain and the United States. In the words of Charles Callan Tansill:

> From the viewpoint of international law the destroyer deal was definitely illegal. As Professor Herbert Briggs correctly remarks: "The supplying of these vessels by the United States Government is a violation of our neutral status, a violation of our national law, and a violation of international law." Professor Edwin Borchard expressed a similar opinion: "To the writer there is no possibility of reconciling the destroyer deal with neutrality, with the United States statutes, or with international law." The whole matter was correctly described by the *St. Louis Post-Dispatch* in a pertinent headline: "Dictator Roosevelt Commits an Act of War" (*Back Door to War*, p.599).

It would be the first of many. Why not? Had he not shown in the prior seven years in office how little he thought of law? For that matter, since he continued to make speeches pledging to stay out of the war, it is perhaps touching to see that FDR's sense of veracity had not altered since the days of the gold confiscation. The president's activities did however cause a rift between him and the Catholic hierarchy.

On February 1, 1941, the US Navy assumed responsibility for protection of British convoys in the Atlantic; on March 11, the Lend-Lease treaty took effect. If ever there were violations of neutrality, these were they. On April 10, 1941, the US destroyer *Niblack,* which was picking up stranded Dutch sailors from their torpedoed ship, dropped depth charges on the submarine which had done the job. After this, as the US ships escorted convoys, there were ever more such incidents.

But Hitler would not rise to the bait. His ships were instructed not to attack if they saw that a ship was American, and only to fire if fired upon. Undeterred, Mr. Roosevelt looked East.

In November, 1940, the Japanese authorities asked Bishop James Walsh of Maryknoll to bring a proposal to Washington; this would include: l) an agreement to end their connection with the Axis, and 2) " a guarantee to recall all military forces from China and to restore to China its geographical and political integrity." His Excellency laid these proposals before FDR and the Secretary of State. He was told they would be taken under advisement. They were never heard of again, much to the chagrin of the Japanese.

After spurning several peace initiatives by Prime Minister Konoye, Roosevelt finally refused to meet with him on August 17, 1941. Finally, stung by his inability to make any arrangement with the US, Prince Konoye resigned on October 16. He was replaced by the less peaceful General Tojo.

On November 15, Secretary of State Cordell Hull handed to the Japanese Ambassador an ultimatum, requiring withdrawal from China. He reiterated those terms on November 26. To a warrior-proud people, who had tried so uncharacteristically long to come to an honorable accord, there seemed, after the final ultimatum, only one way out of the impasse.

The country they were facing across the Pacific had just returned to office for an unprecedented third term Franklin Delano Roosevelt. He was, in November of 1941, at the height of his power. His opponents had failed to unseat him, and those who opposed the warward drift on which he was taking the country were called "Isolationists." Membership in the America First Committee, headed by Col. Charles Lindbergh and John T. Flynn, was considered by many to be tantamount to Fascist Party membership. Yet the Nazis found Roosevelt admirable. According to a *New York Times* dispatch from Berlin (September 26, 1937):

> The German argument contends that democracies like Britain, France, and the United States are inherently weak through lack of an ideology....[However] President Roosevelt in German eyes already is well ahead of world democratic leaders in his perception of the importance of ideology as a factor in national politics....He is believed to be more keenly alive to the post-war necessity of imbuing even democratic formulas with new, even radical spiritual values–less violent and robust maybe than those incorporated in the Fascist and National Socialist decalogues.

Certainly, they should know. The Nazis admired strength above all else, and that FDR had in abundance; he was the living embodiment of the will-to-power, American-style. Leo Gurko's words regarding Huey Long are, one cannot help but feel, even more appropriate for his adversary in the White House:

> What is surprising–and of serious import–is how easily one can be seduced away from the democratic idea; how tyrants, even in America, with its endemic hatred of tyrants, can be glamorized during their lifetime and justified after their death (*The Angry Decade,* p.185).

For Roosevelt was in truth, despite all the Communists and fellow-travelers associated with the New Deal, at heart a Fascist. That may seem a bit harsh; but after all, the American versions of world trends are always softer than the originals. The American and French Revolutions were very close in doctrine, but different in carrying out; the same might be said of Jackson and Bonaparte. So too with Roosevelt and, say, Mussolini. Why are we this way? The temptation is to say simply that we are a nicer bunch of folks than "them foreigners." But it might also be that, as they resist internal subversion much more strongly than we do, perhaps the enemy here need not be so severe. Remember the contrast between Fisher Ames and the Marquis d'Elbee!

At any rate, it were well, before we say farewell to peace-time America, to see what John Flynn had to say about what a Fascist United States would be like:

> Fascism will come at the hands of perfectly authentic Americans, as violently against Hitler and Mussolini as the next one, but who are convinced that the present economic system is washed up and that the present political system in America has outlived its usefulness and who wish to commit this country to the rule of the bureaucratic state; interfering in the affairs of the states and cities; taking part in the management of industry and finance and agriculture; assuming the role of great national banker and investor, borrowing billions every year and spending them on all sorts of projects through which such a government can paralyze opposition and command public support; marshalling great armies and navies at crushing costs to support the industry of war and preparation for war which will become our greatest industry; and adding to all this the most romantic adventures in global planning, regeneration, and domination all to be done under the authority of a powerfully centralized government in which the executive will hold in effect all the powers with Congress reduced to the role of a debating society. There is your fascist. And the sooner America realizes this dreadful fact the sooner it will arm itself to make an end of American fascism masquerading under

the guise of the champion of democracy (*As We Go Marching*, p.253).

What the dogged Mr. Flynn, with his idealism, could not fathom, is that we would love our chains. This is the most recent American Revolution, or at least the penultimate one. We all owe FDR a great debt for it indeed.

But here we have merely spoken of ourselves. The war which Mr. Roosevelt so dearly wished us to enter would change not merely American and world politics, it would alter every element of life, down to the last cuff-link.

See APPENDIX I on p.119 for *The Preamble and Principles of the National Union of Justice.*

BIBLIOGRAPHY

Part I

Diggins, John P., *Mussolini and Fascism: The View From America,* Princeton: Princeton University Press, 1972.

Flynn, John T., *As We Go Marching,* New York: Doubleday, Doran and Co., 1944:

Flynn, John T., *The Roosevelt Myth,* New York: Devin-Adair, 1948.

Foerster, ed., Norman, *Humanism and America,* New York: Farrar and Rinehart, 1930.

Gurko, Leo, *The Angry Decade,* New York: Dodd, Mead, and Co., 1947.

Hicks, John D., *Republican Ascendancy 1921-1933,* New York: Harper and Row, 1960.

Kedward, H.R., *Fascism in Western Europe 1900-1945,* New York: New York University Press, 1971.

Leckie, Robert, *American and Catholic,* Garden City: Doubleday, 1970.

Perrett, Geoffrey, *America in the Twenties,* New York: Simon and Schuster, 1982.

Schriftgiesser, Karl, *This Was Normalcy,* Boston: Little, Brown, and Co., 1948.

Twelve Southerners, *I'll Take My Stand,* New York: Harper and Bros., 1930.

Part II

Agar, Herbert and Tate, Allen, eds., *Who Owns America?,* New York: Houghton Mifflin, 1936, (Willis Fisher, Douglas Jerrold, Hilaire Belloc)

Archer, Jules, *The Plot to seize the White House,* New York: Hawthorn Books, 1973.

Baker, Leonald. *Roosevelt and Pearl Halbor,* New York: Macmillan, 1970.

Bird, Caroline, *The Invisible Scar,* New York: David McKay Co., 1966.

Bocca, Geoffrey, *Kings Without Thrones,* New York: The Dial Press, 1959.

Brinkley, Alan, *Voices of Protest: Huey Long, Father Coughlin, and the Great Depression,* New York: Random House, 1982.

Crane, ed., Milton, *The Roosevelt Era,* New York: Boni and Gaer, 1947.

De Hueck, Baroness Catherine, *Friendship House,* New York: Sheed and Ward, 1946.

Delaney, Edward D., *False Freedom,* Los Angeles: Standard Publications, 1954.

Foot, M.R.D., *Resistance: European Resistance to Nazism 1940-1945,* New York: McGraw-Hill, 1977.

Flynn, John T., *As We Go Marching,* New York: Doubleday, Doran and Co., 1944.

Flynn, John T., *The Roosevelt Myth,* New York: Devin-Adair, 1948.

Foerster, ed., Normall, *Humanism and America,* New York: Farrar and Rinehart, 1930

Garrett, Garet, *The People's Pottage*, Caldwell: The Caxton Printers, 1958.

Gayre, Robert, of Gayre and Nigg, *A Case For Monarchy*, Edinburgh: The Armorial, 1962.

Glaser, Kurt, *Czecho-Slovakia: A Critical History*, Caldwell: The Caxton Printers, 1961

Gregory, Ross, *America 1941*, New York: The Free Press, 1989.

Gurko, Leo, *The Angry Decade*, New York: Dodd, Mead, and Co., 1947.

Halasz, Nicholas, *Roosevelt Throgh Foreign Eyes*, New York: Van Nostrand, 1961.

Hobson, ed., Archie, *Remembering America: A Sampler of the WPA Guide Series*, New York: Columbia University, 1985.

Hoehling, A.A., *Home Front, USA.*, New York: Thomas Y. Crowell, 1966.

Hoopes, Roy, *Americans Remember the Home Front*, New York: Hawthorn Books, 1977.

Jacobsen, Hans-Adolf, *July 20, 1944: Germans Against Hitler*, Bonn: Federal Press and Information Office, 1972.

Josephson, Matthew, *Infidel in the Temple*, New York: Alfred A. Knopf, 1967.

Large, David Clay, *Between Two Fires: Europe's Path in the 1930s*, New York: W.W. Norton and Co., 1990.

Korbonski, Stefan, *Fighting Warsaw*, New York: Funk and Wagnalls, 1968.

Kramarz, Joachim, *Stauffenberg*, New York: Macmillan, 1967.

Lees, Michael, *The Rape of Serbia*, New York: Harcourt Brace Jovanovich, 1990.

Mangione, Jerry, *The Dream and the Deal: The Federal Writers' Project 1935-1943*, Boston: Little, Brown and Co., 1972.

Manly, Chesly, *The Twenty Year Revolution*, Chicago: Henry Regnery Company, 1954.

Maurin, Peter, *Easy Essays*, Chicago: Franciscan Herald Press, 1984.

Miksche, Lt. Col. F.O. *Danubian Federation*, Camberley: privately published, 1953.

Miksche, Lt. Col. F.O. *Unconditional Surrender—The Roots of a World War III*, London: Faber and Faber, 1952.

Nicholls, George Heaton, *South Africa in My Time*, London: Jonathan Cape, 1962.

Nowak, Jan, *Courier From Warsaw*, Detroit: Wayne State University Press, 1982.

Pells, Richard H., *Radical Visions and American Dreams*, New York: Harper and Row, 1973.

Petrie, Sir Charles, *Monarchy in the 20th Century*, London: Andrew Dakers, Ltd., 1952.

Piekalkiewicz, Janusz, *The Cavalry of World War II*, New York: Stein and Day, 1980.

Ready, J. Lee, *Forgotten Allies*, Jefferson, NC: McFarland and Co., 1985.

Ready, J. Lee, *Forgotten Axis*, Jefferson, NC: McFarland and Co., 1984.

Schlabrendorff, Fabian von, *The Secret War Against Hitler*, New York: Pitman Publishing Corp., 1965.

Schmiedeler, Edgar O.S.B., *A Better Rural Life*, New York: Joseph F. Wagner, Inc., 1938.

Schoenbrunn, David, *Soldiers of The Night: The Story of the French Resistance*, New York: E.P. Dutton, 1980.

Snyder, Dr. Louis L., *Encyclopedia of the Third Reich*, New York: Paragon House, 1989.

Swing, Raymond Gram, *Forerunners of American Fascism*, New York: Jilian Messner, 1935.

Tansill, Charles Callan *Back Door to War,* Chicago: Henry Regnery Co., 1952.

Twelve Southerners, *I'll Take My Stand,* New York: Harper and Bros., 1930.

The Unofficial Observer, *The New Dealers,* New York: Simon and Schuster, 1934.

The Unofficial Observer, *American Messiahs,* New York: Simon and Schuster, 1935.

Van Allen, Rodger, *The Commonweal and American Catholicism,* Philadelphia: Fortress Press, 1974.

Viorst, Milton, *Hostile Allies: FDR and De Gaulle,* New York: Macmillan, 1965.

Wedemeyer, Albert C., *Wedemeyer Reports!,* New York: Henry Holt and Co., 1958.

APPENDIX I

The Preamble and Principles of the National Union of Justice

Establishing my principles upon this preamble, namely, that we are all creatures of a beneficent God, made to love and serve Him in this world and to enjoy him forever in the next; and that all this world's wealth of field and forest, of mine and river has been bestowed upon us by a kind Father, therefore, I believe that wealth as we know it originates from the natural resources and from the labor which the sons of God expend upon these resources. It is all ours except for the harsh, cruel, and grasping ways of wicked men who first concentrated wealth into the hands of a few, then dominated states and finally commenced to pit state against state in the frightful catastrophes of commercial warfare.

With this as a preamble, then, these following shall be the principles of social justice towards whose realization we strive.

1. I believe in the right of liberty of conscience and liberty of education, not permitting the state to dictate either my worship to my God or my chosen avocation in life.

2. I believe that every citizen willing to work and capable of working shall receive a just and living annual wage which will enable him to maintain and educate his family according to the standards of American decency.

3. I believe in nationalization of those public necessities which by their very nature are too important to be held in control of private individuals. By these I mean banking, credit and currency, power, light, oil and natural gas and our God-given natural resources.

4. I believe in the private ownership of all other property.

5. I believe in upholding the right to private property yet in controlling it for the public good.

6. I believe in the abolition of the privately owned Federal Reserve Banking system and in the establishment of a Government owned Central Bank.

7. I believe in rescuing from the hands of private owners the right to coin and regulate the value of money, which right must be restored to Congress where it belongs.

8. I believe that one of the chief duties of this Government owned Central Bank is to maintain the cost of living on an even keel and the repayment of dollar debts with equal value dollars.

9. I believe in the cost of production plus a fair profit for the farmer.

10. I believe not only in the right of the laboring man to organize in unions but also in the duty of the Government which that laboring man supports to facilitate and to protect these organizations against the vested interests of wealth and of intellect.

11. I believe in the recall of all non-productive bonds and thereby in the alleviation of taxation.

12. I believe in the abolition of tax exempt bonds.

13. I believe in the broadening of the base of taxation founded upon the ownership of wealth and the capacity to pay.

14. I believe in the simplification of government, and the further lifting of crushing taxation from the slender revenues of the laboring class.

15. I believe that in the event of a war for the defense of our nation and its liberties, there shall be a conscription of wealth as well as a conscription of men.

16. I believe in preferring the sanctity of human rights to the sanctity of property rights. I believe that the chief concern of government shall be for the poor because, as it is witnessed, the rich have ample means of their own to care for themselves.

These are my beliefs. These are the fundamentals of the organization which I present to you under the name of the NATIONAL UNION FOR SOCIAL JUSTICE. It is your privilege to reject or accept my beliefs; to follow me or to repudiate me.